Edward Smith

A history of the schools of Syracuse from its early settlement to

January 1, 1893

Edward Smith

A history of the schools of Syracuse from its early settlement to January 1, 1893

ISBN/EAN: 9783337280031

Printed in Europe, USA, Canada, Australia, Japan

Cover: Foto ©Paul-Georg Meister /pixelio.de

More available books at **www.hansebooks.com**

A HISTORY

OF THE

SCHOOLS OF SYRACUSE

FROM ITS EARLY SET'.

TO

JANUARY 1, 18..

BY

EDWARD SMITH.

SYRACUSE, N. Y.

C. W. BARDEEN, PUBLISHER

1893

CONTENTS

ERRATA

Page 11, 5th line, for *recovered*, read *received*.

Page 13, 4th line, for *Urice*, read *Urico*.

Page 16, last line, for Mr. *May*, read Mr. *Mayo*.

Page 24, line 13, for *Farmton*, read *Taunton*.

Page 194, 7th line from the bottom, for *11,857.91*, read *104,-868.33*.

Page 257, line 14, for ORRIN WELCH, read WILLIAM A. DUNCAN, who was president of the Board that year, and whose name should have been printed in small caps, instead of Mr. Welch's.

Page 262, line 14, for *1874–75 . 2*, read *1874 . 1*.

      "   line 15, for *1876 . 1*, read *1875–76 . 2*.

Page 321, bottom line, for *Mich. Vol. Inf.*, read *Mich. 22d Vol. Inf.*

CONTENTS

(v)

PORTRAITS

VIEWS OF BUILDINGS

(vii)

BIOGRAPHICAL SKETCHES

(viii)

CHAPTER I

EARLY BEGINNINGS

———

From long connection with the schools of this city, and a somewhat familiar acquaintance with the educational interests of the county and the State, the writer has yielded to suggestions from several sources, and decided to prepare a brief history of the public educational work of Syracuse.

Coming upon the ground early in the spring of 1845 for the purpose of visiting a brother, then living in the village of Syracuse, and, hearing of a vacancy in the village, district No. 8 of Salina, I made application to the trustees of that district for employment as teacher. A bargain was made and contract signed for school to begin the first Monday in May. From that time to the present, I have been constantly employed in the educational work of this city, with the exception of three summers from 1857 to 1860, returning to teach during the winters of those years. Hence I hope to be able to put on permanent record something that may be valuable to those of the present generation who take an interest in this subject, and to preserve for future generations that which from the lapse of years and the decease of participants it will soon be impossible otherwise to collect. Even at this date, it is difficult to find records of many of the transactions which would be of interest, and I am compelled to rely upon the recollection of those who were actors in the early days of the education of this vicinity. Only a few are now on the stage to whom application can be made.

From the best data obtainable, I think the first district school organized within the present city limits was in the village of Geddes, which by act of the Legislature was annexed to the city in 1887. The school house was built in 1804. But little can be learned of the early teachers of that school. After my acquaintance with it Mr. and Mrs. N. P. Stanton were the leading teachers in that district. and Mr. E. W. Curtis was school commissioner. Mr. Curtis was enthusiastic in his efforts to make the school where he resided stand among the first of the county, and Mr. Stanton was a popular and energetic teacher. Of some of the teachers more will be said hereafter.

Schools were taught at an early date, without doubt, in private houses at what was known as Salt Point, now the First Ward of the city, and one Capt. Connor kept school in a salt block, where he divided his time between teaching and salt boiling. The Onondaga Centennial Almanac, published in 1886, says this was about 1797.

Gov. Thomas G. Alvord, now living in the First Ward, says that Salina had 63 inhabitants when his father moved into the place, in 1793. Several items of interest connected with the early history of this village have been obtained from Gov. Alvord.

The first school house within what were the limits of the city when it recovered its charter was built in the village of Salina, now the First Ward of the city, in 1805. It was at first seated with the faces of the pupils toward the wall, according to the fashion of those days, but was afterward changed for pupils to face the centre of the room, where the stove was placed with the teacher's table at the end of the room, by the entrance. The town of Salina was incorporated in 1809, and this, being the first organized district, was designated No. 1.

It was located in the south-western corner of Washington Park, while the Presbyterian church, built in 1822, was on the north-west corner. The school house was probably re-built at a later day, painted red, and known as the Red School House. The village of Salina was incorporated in 1824, but this school remained as No. 1 of the town of Salina until the city of Syracuse was incorporated in 1848. Among its teachers were Mr. West, Mr. Stebbins, Mr. Gilbert, Walter Green, a brother of the late Dr. Green, Thomas Wheeler, David Devoe, and others.

In 1839 this district was divided, the old building having been torn down by the boys as unfit for school purposes, and two one-story brick buildings were erected

Schoolhouse in District No. 8, Salina, as it now appears. When the author became principal, the building consisted of the lower story as far back as to include three windows on a side.

on Wolf street, three blocks apart, and known as No. 1, or the Bank school, and No. 8.

Among the later teachers of the new No. 1 were David Parsons, Urice Henry Van Seest. Lewis Cornell ; and of No. 8, Thomas Wheeler, Mr. Whitney, David Parsons, Elijah Devoe, and the writer, who began teaching in May, 1845.

After I was employed I visited the school building, and found it seated with two rows of long desks, about three feet apart, fastened to the floor, with movable benches between. The desks were about eleven feet in length and the inconvenience of seating pupils was so great that I obtained permission to cut up the desks into shorter ones of three and a half feet in length, and arrange them in rows with a passage between. On my offer to help in the work a carpenter was employed, and in a short time the room was made comfortable, and by planing out the notches and applying a coat of paint the desks were made quite respectable. Two pupils were to be seated at a desk.

Although the house had been occupied only a few years it had been badly disfigured by a free use of pocket-knives, and from being used for temperance meetings, singing schools, spelling schools, and political meetings, etc., sometimes two or even more times a week ; and for election purposes, both State and local. But when the new term began the seats had been put in very good condition.

The spring term opened with about fifty pupils of all grades in the elementary studies, the greater part of them small children. The winter brought in the older pupils, many of them much larger than the teacher. These new pupils increased the number to over 100, and an assistant, Miss A. Bennett, was employed. As there was only one room, the wood-house was utilized for recitations, a part of it having a floor. The numbers increased so that it became necessary to seat some of the pupils on the wood-pile.

During the second summer one teacher was employed, and the wood-house was made into a very comfortable school room by putting in windows and a new floor, proper shelter for fuel being provided outside. At the opening of the winter term an assistant was again employed. This arrangement continued till the schools passed under the control of the Board of Education of the city in the spring of 1848.

Previous to this the village had been again divided, and two other schools organized. No. 15 was under the charge of Mr. J. B. Brigham, lately deceased, and No. 16 was taught by Miss Delia N. Earl. Miss Earl later decided to go to California, where she married after teaching a while. Mr. Lewis Cornelle had charge of school No. 1 when the city was organized.

The first school house in the village of Syracuse was one on Church street (West Willow), on ground now

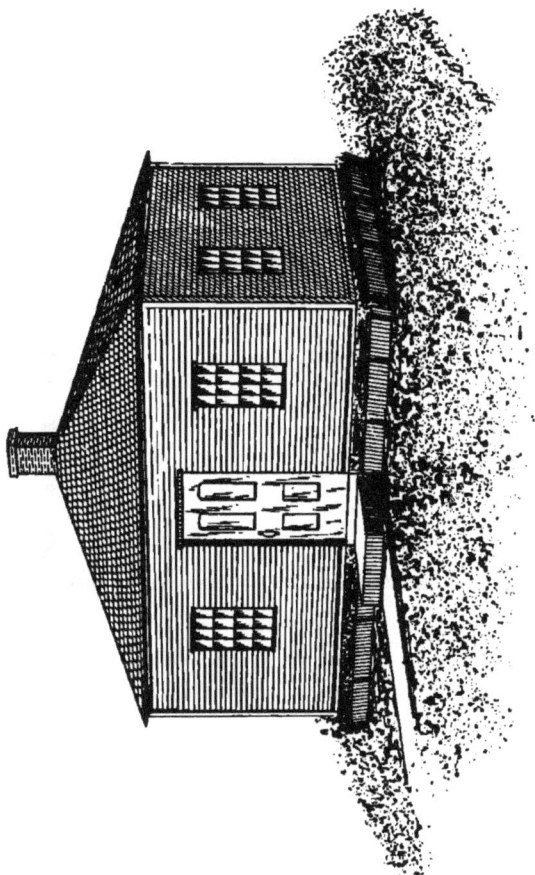

The first schoolhouse in Syracuse.

occupied by Mr Young's stables, corner of Church and Franklin streets.   Probably this was built about 1826.*

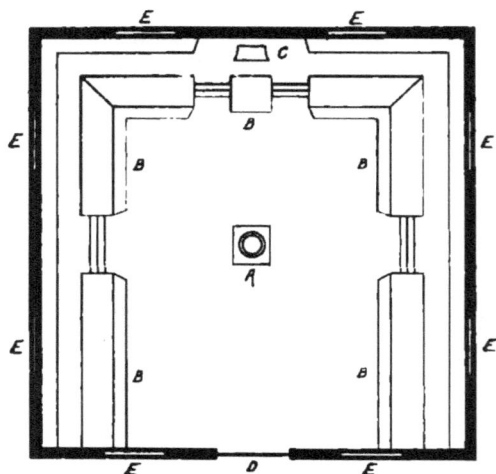

A - STOVE .
B - SCHOLARS DESKS .
C - TEACHER'S DESK .
D - ENTRANCE .
E - WINDOWS .

Interior plan of first schoolhouse.

It was a square hip-roof building, and was used for school, church, town meetings and various other purposes.   Among the teachers were Wm. K. Blair, Mr. Williams, Hiram A. Dunham, Mr. Evans, Mr. May,

* There is doubt about the date of this building.   Miss E. M. Shepard now a resident in the Tenth Ward says she attended a school in 1826 near the lock taught by Miss Pease, and there was no district school in Syracuse at that time.

and others who did excellent work and from whom many of the early settlers received their education either wholly or in part.

District No. 5 was organized January 1, 1839, on Lock street. Jerod H. Parker was the moderator, Wm. K. Blair the clerk. E. F. Wallace, J. H. Parker and S. W. Cadwell were the first trustees. Several school meetings followed each other in rapid succession during the winter and spring. A lot fronting on Lock and Salt streets was purchased, plans approved, and a contract let for a house to cost $1,600. Elliot & Cheney were the contractors. A tax list for $2,000 was made out and put into the collector's hands, but the whole amount could not be realized and the building was not entirely completed.

At the annual meeting in October there was reported a school kept six months (name of teacher not given). This building was too small, and the next year and the following year's efforts to enlarge and improve it finally resulted in putting up a two-story front, with four more rooms. This was the building when the city received its charter.

Among those prominent as actors in this work beside those named above were E. W. Leavenworth, F. Colvin, L. L. D., James Hough, John A. Leonard, father of George B. Leonard of this city, John Wilkinson, Milton Gilbert and John C. Dunham, with others. Among the early teachers were Mr. Hunt, Mr. Penniman, David Parsons, U. H. Van Seest, and Mr. Stetson.

District No. 6 contained a one-story brick building of two rooms situated on West Fayette street. It was afterward enlarged by an addition in the rear to a three-room building. The old mill pond came near it on the west, and covered a large part of the territory west and south of it, comprising all the low land where Armory Park and the surrounding buildings now stand. When the writer came here in 1845, Mr. Sloan was the principal, with one assistant. This house was abandoned when Madison school house was built in 1872. Although unoccupied for school purposes for a number of years it was used for a laundry later, and stood till a block was put up on the ground in 1890 or 1891.

The first school building in District No. 7 was of brick, one story and one room with two entrances and a small room between them. It was built in 1839 on the ground occupied by the old Putnam school, which was abandoned in 1888 for school purposes when the new Putnam house was completed.

A Mr. Osgood, nephew of Capt. Putnam, was the first teacher. He was a graduate from college, but he did not succeed. A Miss Phelps, sister of Mr. Bradley Carey, probably assisted Mr. Osgood. Mr. A. G. Salisbury followed Mr. Osgood after a few months, assisted

ALBERT G. SALISBURY.

by Mary Bradley and Sarah Tallman, who afterward married Mr. Salisbury. Miss Tallman used the small room between the entrances for recitations.

SARAH TALLMAN.
(MRS. A. G. SALISBURY.)

The school house was the best in the vicinity, and when it was built was considered quite an ornament to the growing village. But it was soon found wholly inadaquate to meet the necessities of the pupils who desired to attend. A wooden addition was annexed to the rear, by which some relief was obtained. In 1842 an effort was made to secure a better house, Dr. Phillips, Dr. Wright, and Horace Butts being trustees at that time. The matter was presented to the people, and two parties were formed. One headed by Capt. Putnam was in favor of a good school, good house, with sufficient room; and the other, led by Mr. Richard Corning, favored economy and lower taxes.

The progressive party were successful, and in 1843 the building was completed. To the old structure a two-story brick front with two rooms on a floor was added on the south end, and the wooden part previously annexed to the north end was removed and a brick addition erected. The building when completed had five rooms, and was far superior to any other school house in the county.

Mr. Salisbury about this time taught a select school in the session room of the Congregational church. This may have been while No. 7 was being enlarged. After the new structure was completed Mr. Salisbury continued as principal till he was elected clerk of the Board of Education, after Syracuse became a city in the Spring of 1848. He had secured a practical grading of pupils and made the school popular in the village.

District No. 9 had a small one-room wood building, situated on West street.

. No. 10 located in the village of Lodi had a small house situated on East Genesee street, probably built first in 1828. The first teacher was a Mr. Parker, followed by a Mr. Brown. This was replaced in 1846 by a two-story brick building on East Fayette street, containing four rooms, known as the "Cold Water School." The late Oliver Teall was the leader in this movement and was greatly interested in the success of his temperance movement, as he was in the education of the children of the district. Mr. Gordon Rose was a teacher before 1848.

This comprises all the public schools included in the limits of the city of Syracuse at its organization in 1848, but the city now includes much more school property.

The town of Geddes was formed from the town of Salina in 1848, the same year the city of Syracuse received its charter. The village of Geddes was incorporated in the winter of 1835–36. Previous to 1848 it was a village in the town of Salina. The first settler within the town was James Geddes, who came there in 1794, almost a hundred years ago.

In 1803 Miss Nancy Root taught the first school in Geddes. The first schoolhouse was built of logs in 1804 on the ground occupied by the Porter school.

Miss E. M. Shepard, now a resident in the village of Geddes (10th Ward), has given me more information than I have been able to obtain from other sources of the early schools of Geddes and vicinity. She attended a school, taught by Mrs. Pease, near the lock (Syracuse) in her own house in 1826, and in 1827–28 attended a school in Lodi (she does not remember the teacher's name). A schoolhouse was built in Lodi in 1828, and, occupied by Mr. Parker as teacher, continued two years. In 1830 a Mr. Brown was employed, and Mr. Parker had a select school.

In 1831 Miss Shepard removed to Geddes, and in 1832–33 she attended a school in the basement of the Episcopal Church, kept by Mr. Younglove. In the

PORTER SCHOOL.

spring of 1833 Miss Shepard taught a select school in her own house, now the corner of West Genesee street and Avery avenue. In 1835, she assisted Mr. Terry in a small brick house at the corner of School and Lowell streets ; and assisted Mr. Bugby in the basement of the Episcopal Church in 1834, while Mr. Terry was teaching in the public school the same year. In the winter of 1837 she assisted Mr. Austin, on the north side of Genesee street, near Milton avenue.

Miss Shepard attended the academy in Elbridge during the summer term of 1839, and taught the district school there in 1840–41, when failing health caused her to discontinue the work. Farmton, Howlett Hill and Amboy were among the other places in this vicinity where she taught.

For other teachers we gather from more full records than any obtainable from schools in the city at its organization.

The first branch of the old No. 3 of the town of Geddes was organized in 1867, and a scoolhouse was built on Magnolia street and named Noble school, in honor of the late Mr. W. Noble, who was thoroughly interested in the education of the young. He was clerk of the board at the time and was very earnest in his efforts in securing an appropriation for the purpose. After several years the name was changed to Magnolia school, perhaps owing in part to its being located on that street.

The first principal was a Miss Robinson, assisted by Miss Garrett and Miss Sarah Jerome, now Mrs. —— Parsons, of Fairmount. Miss Jerome succeeded to the principalship in 1868, and held it two years, when she accepted a position in the senior department of No. 3, or as it was afterwards called, the Central school, where she remained three years, and then married.

Miss Hattie Tucker, now Mrs. Charles Coykendal, followed Miss Jerome as principal, and remained until 1874, when she accepted a position in Montgomery school and remained there two years. At the time Miss Tucker resigned the village schoolhouse had been rebuilt, and the older pupils who had attended the Magnolia school were transferred to the new building. Miss Nellie Annable, now Mrs. Henry Smith, followed as principal for a short time, and was succeeded by Mrs. Libbie McKaig. The other principals were Miss Mary Van Franken, who married Mr. Fred Thompson; Miss Ella

JENNIE E. WHITE.

Scanlon, whose health failed and who died before the year closed; Miss Joanna C. Ryan, now Mrs. Ed. Grainey, of Washington, followed for one year by Miss Jennie E. White, who continued for nine years and until the Magnolia school was abandoned and the Delaware school completed in the spring of 1890, where she is now principal of the primary department.

What is now known as the Frazer school, second branch of Porter school, was organized by the Board of Education of the village of Geddes in 1879. The house was of wood and stood on the ground now occupied by the present 10-room brick building, the wooden structure having been burned in 1885. The new building was erected and occupied in 1887. The tract of land known as the Cushendall tract, the territory of which was included in this district, was added to the city of Syracuse in the spring of 1886, the schools being maintained in rented rooms until the new house was completed.

The first school opened under the supervision of Mary E. Hogan, assisted by Franc C. Chamberlain. Miss Hogan is now teaching in Hartford, Conn. Miss Chamberlain married and went west.

The Rock school was first organized in Geddes in 1872. It opened in a building at 92 Geddes street, owned by a Mr. Steele, and was kept by Miss Clara L. Cowles. Two years later the district purchased the Brown Memorial chapel, then located where the pres-

FRAZER SCHOOL.

OLD ROCK SCHOOLHOUSE.

ent church stands, removed it to Rock street, and converted into what was called the "Rock School." Miss Cowles remained only a few terms, but taught in other Geddes schools, and then went west. She remained there till 1887, when she returned to her home, where she now lives near her first school work. The other teachers of this school will be found in the list that appears later.

The origin of the Brighton school was district No. 44, of the town of Onondaga, which was organized in 1842 with Matthias Britton as trustee. Mr. Britton was continued in this office nearly all the time till the district became a part of the city. The first schoolhouse was built of stone, one story high. It was low and small, but it accomodated the district until 1860, when a two-story brick building was erected and served the district until the new Brighton schoolhouse was occupied in 1891. The district became a part of the city in 1887.

Instead of raising a tax to build the first house, interested citizens contributed what they could toward the expense, some giving money, some material for the building, and some labor. Among the early teachers were J. L. Hibbard, brother-in-law of Mr. Britton, Sherman Olmsted, Joseph Longstreet, Sophia Wightman, C. Clark, Wm. Thompson, H. Wilcox, L. Burton. After the brick house was built two teachers and sometimes three were employed. A list of the other teachers will be found later.

OLD BRIGHTON SCHOOL.

BRIGHTON SCHOOL.

In 1863 the district was changed to Union Free School, District No. 2, town of Onondaga, and a Board of Education composed of six members was elected.

School District No. 29 of the town of Onondaga was founded June 17, 1878, from the north part of Union Free School, District No. 2, of that town, and comprised all the territory included in the limits of the incorporated village of Danforth, and known as the Union Free School of that village. The first principal was Leon Bailey, assisted by Miss R. Angie Lounsbury and Julia E. Phelps. Miss Phelps resigned to accept a position in the city schools, and was succeeded by Miss Louise Burdick, who also resigned in December and was followed by Miss Jennie White. December 23, 1879, Principal Bailey was asked to resign. He did not comply, but was discharged on December 31, and Mr. P. H. Edick was appointed to the principalship.

In July, 1880, Miss Josie Wightman was appointed in the primary department, but resigned the following spring, as also did Miss Lounsbury. Mr. Edick resigned to go to Chittenango. He afterward became superintendent of schools at Owego, and is now principal of a school in Rochester. H. A. Thompson was elected principal in May, 1881, and Miss Louise Roberts was elected teacher in the primary department.

Mr. Thompson resigned at the close of the summer term and was succeeded by W. F. Barker, Miss Carrie Ingersol and Miss May Hitchings being appointed assistants.

EBENEZER BUTLER.

In July, 1882, Ebenezer Butler succeeded Mr. Barker. Miss May Morse entered the school as an assistant in the fall of 1883 ; and Miss Minnie Smith succeeded Miss Ingersol at the same time, but resigned the following summer and was followed by Miss Ella Thompson. Miss Lulu Leyden was appointed in the spring of 1885, and in September of the same year Miss May Van Keuren took the place of Miss Morse. Miss Mary Northrup was added to the corps of teachers, September, 1886. There were no other changes in teachers till after the village of Danforth was annexed to the city of Syracuse in February, 1887, when the name was changed to Danforth school.

I have not been able to get the exact date of the formation of the Rose school. It was probably 1810 or 12, and the first house was built of logs at the foot of a hill on land owned by Wheeler Rose. The roof was a single one, sloping all one way, and it is said the boys amused themselves in winter by sliding down the hill and over the roof of the house. The house which succeeded the first one stood where the Rose school was located when the district became a part of the city. The district was among the first in this part of the county, there being none nearer than Jamesville or Onondaga Valley. Pupils were obliged to travel two or three miles to reach the school.

We should not do justice to the educational interests of the city if the private and select schools and the in-

Rose School.

fluence of the academies were to be omitted in this enumeration.

The first district schoolhouse in this vicinity was built of logs at Onondaga Valley, in 1803, and replaced with a frame building in 1808.

Onondaga academy was founded in 1813, and many of the young men in the early settlement of this place attended there and received thorough instruction which prepared them for business life.

The people of Pompey made an effort as early as 1800 to found an academy, and continued trying year after year till finally success crowned their efforts in 1811. This institution has sent out many men of influence in all departments of labor, and this city, especially in its early history, has been indebted to its graduates for much that has shaped its educational influence and standing.

It has been with considerable difficulty that reliable data could be found respecting all the private and select schools that have had a more or less permanent influence upon the condition of education within the limits of our city, and undoubtedly some have been omitted or perhaps not adequately reported.

In 1826 a Miss Wealthy Ann Lathrop taught a select school in a building provided by Captain Cody, in the rear of the First Baptist church, on Church street. (This church was established in 1821, and was the first

church built in Syracuse.) This is said to have been
the first select school in the village. In 1830, Miss
Guthrie had a select school in the Wheeler house, corner of Salina and Centre streets. There was also a
school known as the Institute, situated on Tuttle street,
between Park and Salina streets, which had some reputation for several years.

In 1835. George F. Comstock, lately deceased. taught
in the yellow building standing where the Bastable
Block now is. He was elected Inspector of Schools in
1837.

The Misses Champlain taught the principal private
school in existence here for a few years. As there was
a difficulty in finding suitable rooms, Dr. Williams
put up a temporary building on the corner of Water
and Clinton streets. Mrs. Humphrey followed in
charge of this school. The house built by Mr. Williams, being without ceiling or plaster, was unfit for
winter use, and Captain Putnam fitted up for Mrs.
Humphrey a more comfortable room over his woodshed,
on Montgomery street. This was known as Montgomery Institute. Mrs. Humphrey and Mr. Montgomery afterward married. After Mrs. Montgomery. came
Miss Richardson, Miss Alexander, Mrs. Newcomb, the
Misses Newton from Massachusetts, Mrs. Col. Fitch
from Trumansburg, Miss Collins, Miss Laurie from
Whitesboro, and Miss Gould from South Carolina.
Most of these named above were teachers of a high

order, some of them teaching the sciences, higher mathematics and the languages.

Probably about 1838, a Miss Parrott of Kentucky came here with credentials from prominent men, among them Henry Clay. This lady and T. D. Williams opened a school called The Young Ladies' Seminary, about midway between Water and Washington streets on the west side of Salina street, which continued two or three years, during which time Mr. Williams and Miss Parrott married. The school then moved to the Old Line House, corner of Salina and West Onondaga streets, which was at that time considered quite suburban. Many of the young ladies of the village were students in this Seminary.

Miss Amelia Bradbury entered the school as an assistant in 1838. She introduced new methods and new inspiration. She believed and worked on the principle that character-building is of vastly more importance than scholarly acquirement. She instituted self-government, appealed to the moral sense of the young ladies, encouraged frankness and candor, and in the pursuit of their studies sought to inspire in her pupils the power to investigate for themselves. She was modest and unpretentious and soon won the respect and admiration of her pupils. Such became her popularity that she was induced to open a school of her own, which she did in the Unitarian chapel, where Mr. Brower's establishment now is. She remained in this school from 1845 to 1847. Debora Garnett, now the widow of Hon. Charles B. Sedgwick, taught in the same school, and testifies to the excellence of Miss Bradbury's methods.

Miss Bradbury died in 1850. Miss Palmer, who afterward married Ira A. Thurber, opened a school in the Jervis Block, giving it the name of The Young Ladies' Seminary. After her marriage, she sold the fixtures to George L. Farnham, who kept up the school until he was elected superintendent of the public schools of the city. His portrait is given on the next page.

The Syracuse Academy was organized in 1835 by Aaron Burt, Harvey Baldwin and Oliver Teal. The first principal was a Mr. Kellogg from New York. He was followed by Oren Root, afterwards professor of mathematics in Hamilton College ; A. G. Salisbury, already referred to on page 18 ; Joseph A. Allen, afterwards one of the most notable teachers of Massachusetts ; Oliver P. Burt, and perhaps others. The Academy proved a financial failure and was abandoned. The premises were sold to the Onondaga County Orphan Asylum, which now occupies the premises, having within a few years removed the old edifice and erected upon the grounds a new and more commodious and improved building. Syracuse Academy was in operation only ten or eleven years, but during its short life it did excellent work.

Many of the teachers enumerated above had attained a high degree of culture, and employed methods of

GEORGE L. FARNHAM.

instruction which far surpassd the average of those
employed in the common district school ; and to them
is due, largely, that public sentiment which has enabled
the city schools to take and maintain, through all its
history, a forward movement toward a more thorough
system of education and more philosophical methods,
until we believe it may be said of them they deserve
to be ranked among the first of the land.

CHAPTER II

UNDER CITY SUPERVISION

So far an effort has been made to present the condition at the organization of the public schools maintained at public expense under the charge of a Board of Education.

The village of Syracuse was laid out into streets and lots in 1819, but the first election of village officers occurred in 1825. The first schoolhouse was erected in 1820, the first church (Baptist) was built in 1821, and the First Presbyterian church in 1824. The first grist mill occupied the ground where the high school now stands, the building itself standing well into the street. The village of Lodi consisted of a cluster of houses, groceries, etc., situated on the canal east of Syracuse, along by the locks.

During the winter of 1847–48 the project of incorporating the three villages (Salina, Lodi and Syracuse) into a city began to be discussed. Meetings were held and arguments for and against a city charter were freely made. Those favorably inclined were in the majority, and the result was a bill before the Legislature which became a law, Dec. 14, 1847. The election for city officers resulted in making Harvey Baldwin the first mayor. Two aldermen were chosen for each of the four wards into which the city had been divided, as follows :

First Ward, James Lynch, Elizur Clark.

Second Ward, Alexander McKinstry, John B. Burnett.

Third Ward, Wm. H. Alexander, Gardner Lawrence.

Fourth Ward, H. W. Durnford, Robert Furman.

The first one named in each of the wards was to serve two years and the other one year. The first meeting of the common council was held March 13, 1848, and organized by electing R. A. Yoe city clerk, and the late Daniel P. Wood city attorney. Dr. B. F. Greene was made city surveyor, and Dr. Hiram Hoyt, city physician. None of them, except R. A. Yoe, are now living.

The act of incorporation was found to be defective in several particulars, and among others that pertaining to a system of public schools. During the remainder of the month of March and the fore part of April, petitions, following each other as the deficiencies were made apparent, were sent to the Legislature for immediate action. As a result an act for organizing a public school system in the city of Syracuse was passed April 11, 1848, and certified to the Common Council at a meeting held April 15. According to the provisions of the charter the Common Council, at a meeting held April 15, appointed two school commissioners from each of the wards, who were to constitute the Board of Education of the city of Syracuse. The first one named in each ward was to serve two years, and the other one year. Choice was made of prominent business men, viz.:

William Clark and John P. Babcock, for the *First Ward*.

James Noxon and C. M. Bronson, for the *Second Ward*.

Hiram Putnam and Daniel Bradley, for the *Third Ward*.

Oliver Teal and Charles A. Wheaton, for the *Fourth Ward*.

The meeting for organizing the Board was held April 21. William Clark was elected the first president but declined to serve, and Hiram Putnam was elected to this responsible position. He proved to be eminently fitted for the trust committed to him, and his sympathies were all on the side of good schools and the best possible equipments. He was kind and generous in his impulses, but firm. Having made up his mind as to the right or wrong of a question he could not be shaken.

Mr. R. A. Yoe acted as temporary clerk. A committee of three was appointed to present rules for the government of the Board, and the same committee with the addition of two other members were to present a report of the duties of the clerk of the Board of Education. All commissioners were to report the number of teachers it would be necessary to appoint at the next meeting of the Board. The second meeting was held April 26, at which the committees appointed at the preceding one made full reports, but as the reports did not harmonize in every respect they were recommitted for revision.

At this meeting A. G. Salisbury (see pages 19, 21), was elected the first clerk, having received 5 votes. His opponent was E. C. Pomeroy. Both of these gentlemen were thorough and successful teachers, but Mr. Salisbury was on the ground and had been identified with the village schools for several years, while Mr. Pomeroy was comparatively a stranger.

Mr. Salisbury was regarded as a strict disciplinarian and a thorough teacher. He was popular among his patrons. A more scrupulously conscientious man could hardly be found. In many respects he was well fitted for a supervisor and director, and his services as clerk, though not continued for a great length of time, revealed his power and influence by opening up and starting the machinery of the school system of the city.

At this second meeting a resolution was adopted declining to appoint any person as teacher who habitually used intoxicating drinks or tobacco. Applications for appointment as teachers in the newly organized schools were made in writing by Messrs. Scram, Beal,

Slocum, Cornell, Goodrich, Johnston, and Brigham.
Four of these persons were known to the writer as eminently fitted for teachers. Three ladies also made
application. After an adjournment of two days the
Board again met to hear the report of the committee on
rules and duties of clerk. The report was adopted.
The appointment of teachers was postponed till the
Common Council should make necessary appropriation
for meeting the current expenses of the schools. Some
needed repairs to school buildings were however ordered
to be charged to the city.

On May 2, another meeting was held, at which the
school year was divided into three terms : the 1st to
begin May 8, and continue 13 weeks ; the 2d to begin
September 18, and continue 14 weeks ; the 3d to begin
January 2, and continue 14 weeks.

The first appointment of teachers with the monthly
salary of each was also made, as follows :

District No.	1, Lewis Cornelle,	$35
" "	8, Edward Smith,	35
" "	15, John B. Brigham,	30
" "	16, James Johonnot,	35
	Delia N. Earl,	15
" "	4, N. P. Stanton,	45
	Mrs. N. P. Stanton,	18
	Miss Palmer,	15
" "	5, R. R. Stetson,	45
	Mrs. R. R. Stetson,	16

District No. 5, Miss Martha S. Clapp, $18
                 Miss Julia A. Vandenburg,   18
    "   "   6, J. B. Beals,   35
                 Miss Hannah Burnett,   15
    "   " 20, Miss A. Bennett,   18
    "   "   7, W. W. Newman,   50
                 Miss E. E. Williams,   18
                 Miss E. Williams,   15
                 Miss J. Brooks,   18
                 Miss S. M. Cox,   18
                 Miss R. C. Newman,   18
    "   " 10, J. M. Winchell,   35
                 Miss A. Barker,   15
                 Miss H. Kingsley,   18

Twenty-four teachers with a combined total salary of
$5,980, with ten school buildings, four of them having
only one room, two others having two rooms, and No.
7, the largest, employing six teachers : such was the
beginning of the Syracuse schools.   At the next meeting of the Board steps were taken for building the first
new schoolhouse.   A committee was appointed to choose
a lot, make plans for a building in place of No. 16 (now
called Jefferson school), in the First Ward, and during
the building of the new house to rent rooms and seat
them with the best furniture, such as would be fit to
put into the new house when it should be ready for
occupancy.

Two or three meetings a week were held during the
organization of the schools at which, in addition to

what has already been recorded, the standing committees were appointed, viz.: executive, finance, teachers'
and visiting. Resolutions passed required at the opening of the morning session either reading of the Script-
ures or a prayer as the teacher should elect; the
providing of books for all indigent pupils; the choice
of a series of books for school use; the purchase of a
lot for the new building for No. 16, on the corner of
Court and Salt (now Park) streets; the adoption of
plans and the letting the contract for the building, the
entire cost, including lot, to be $3,000.

On June 15, 1848, the first budget for school expenses
was prepared and presented to the Common Council.
The estimates were for teachers' salaries, $5,664; for
contingent expenses, $1,450; for Clerk of Board of
Education, $500; for books for indigent pupils, $100;
for repairs, $100; for lights, fuel, etc., $75; for printing, $50. The entire expenses, including building,
lot, etc., made a total of $11,160.

At a meeting of the Board, July 12, it was decided to
close the schools August 2 instead of the 5th that teachers might be able to attend the New York State Teachers' Association at Auburn. This institution had been
organized three years before in this city and had already
become a power for good in the educational centres of
the State.

The rule requiring the reading of the Bible at the
opening of the morning session, passed at a preceding

meeting, had caused some opposition, and much discussion through the summer and fall. It was finally settled, October 4, by changing the original resolution so as to permit the children of parents or guardians who should object, to be absent without criticism during such reading.

The numbers by which the schools had been designated were given to them while belonging to the town of Salina, but at a meeting in October these were changed to consecutive numbers, 1 to 10 inclusive. The resignation of Mr. Beal from No. 6 was accepted and Mr. McGonegal was appointed to the position.

No. 7 had been increasing during the summer so that addition to teachers became necessary and the Misses Harriet Shane and Sarah Wilkinson were appointed. Miss Wilkinson died in Skaneateles in September, 1892.

A complaint against Principal Stetson, for punishing a boy, was investigated. He was exonerated for inflicting the punishment, but reproved for sending home the books of other children of the family. A similar complaint against Principal Winchell resulted in his exoneration. Another against Principal McGonegal for inconsiderate, injudicious, and unjustifiable conduct in punishing a boy was decided against the teacher, and led to his dismissal.

In December a warrant for $3,000 was drawn in favor of Congdon and Carey in full for their contracts for

JEFFERSON SCHOOL.

the building and lot No. 16 (changed to No. 3).
This entirely finished the payment of the first lot and
schoolhouse built by the city of Syracuse.

The resignation of Mr. N. P. Stanton and wife from
No. 4 was accepted. Mr. Stanton had received an
appointment to a principalship in Buffalo, which was a
much larger city and offered a higher salary. By this
resignation, Syracuse lost two excellent teachers.

A request from the teachers for a change on the
ground of want of uniformity in the different editions
of Sanders' Readers, was presented to the Board, but
was declined upon the agreement of the author to take
up all old editions, free of charge, and replace them
with the revised edition.

February 19, 1849, the first Annual Report of the
Board of Education was presented, and was referred to
the committee to prepare for publication. . It contained
the following statistics:

Number of schools, - - - 10
Number of children of school age, - 3,724
Number of children taught during the year, 3,250
Number in daily average attendance, 1,201
Money received from the city, $ 7,318.00
Money received from other sources, 5,213.60
Total, - - - 12,531.60
Number of children taught in excess of pre-
     ceding year, - - - 675
Seating accommodations, - - - 1,460

Excess of pupils of school age over accommodations,   -   -   -   2,264

Excess of pupils not registered in parochial
schools,   -   -   -   - 2,091

Of the ten schools, nine were presided over by men
principals having salaries ranging from $30 to $60 per
month, with 15 women teachers, at salaries ranging
from $15 to $20 per month.

Total cost of teachers' wages,   - $7,602.48

Cost of tuition per pupil on average attendance,   -   -   -   -   6.31

Cost of tuition per pupil on registered
attendance,   -   -   -   2.33

Cost of building No. 3 (now Jefferson
school)   -   -   -   3,000.

The average attendance of pupils to a teacher was 50.

The report strongly urged the erection of new buildings in the 2d, 3d and 4th wards, and the enlargement
of the house in District No. 6. It presented the work
of the department in a concise and comprehensive manner and made clear the advantages systematic grading
and supervision had secured to the city schools.

Commissioners J. P. Babcock, C. M. Bronson, Daniel Bradley, Oliver Teal and Charles A. Wheaton
retired from the Board after one year's service, and they
were succeeded by Dr. Wm. H. Hoyt, Ira A. Thurber,
Rev. Robert R. Raymond, J. B. Fitch and Dr. P. C.
Samson.

The second school year was opened by the organization of the Board, March 12. 1849, in which Captain Putnam was re-elected president and A. G. Salisbury, clerk. An effort was made to reduce Nos. 1, 2 and 8 to primary schools, and have women teachers appointed in the place of men, but this was defeated by a vote of 5 to 3. The appointment of teachers, made in April, by wards, was as follows :

First Ward.

G. N. Harris,	principal,	No.	1
Mary E. Grodevant,	"	"	2
Edward Smith,	"	"	8
James Johonnot,*	"	"	3
Delia N. Earll,	assistant	"	3
Harriet Davis,	"	"	3

Second Ward.

R. R. Stetson,	principal,	No.	5
Martha S. Clapp,	assistant,	"	
Jane Vandenburg,	"	"	
Mrs. R. R. Stetson,	"	"	
D. Caverno Allen,	principal,	No.	4
Helen Palmer,	assistant,	"	
Harriet Pomeroy,	principal,	No.	9

Third Ward.

George B. Dennison, principal, No. 7

---

* Mr. Johonnot's appointment was conditioned upon his dissolving his connection with the *Literary Union*, which Messrs. Winchell and Johonnot had started as an educational magazine.

Emma Williams,   assistant, No. 7
Sarah Williams,   "   "
Angelina Butts,   "   "
Elizabeth Williams,   "   "
C. R. McCombs,   "   "

Fourth Ward.

Lewis Cornelle,   principal, No. 6
Hannah Burnett,   assistant,   "
J. B. Brigham,   principal, No. 10
Mary Baum,   assistant,   "

On account of a protest against Principal Brigham's appointment in No. 2 he was transferred to No. 10, and complaints having been made against W. W. Newman he withdrew from No. 7, the Board by resolution having vindicated his character from the assaults made upon it. Later in the summer at Mr. Newman's request a paper signed by the president and clerk was prepared for him, stating that Mr. Newman was not dismissed from No. 7 for infidelity or any cause affecting his moral character.

At a meeting in May of this year a resolution was passed fixing the first Thursday as the regular time for holding the meetings of the Board. This regulation has continued in force until the present time without change.

In October of this year Mr. Johonnot was charged with undue severity and indiscretion, and Mr. Stetson was under criticism for extending a leave of absence

W. W. NEWMAN.

beyond the time specified. Both of these cases were amicably settled. From these cases and those mentioned as having occurred the year before, it will be noticed as of common occurrence for the Board to receive complaints against teachers for punishment inflicted and for various other causes. This continued for several years, although with less frequency.

The salary of the principal of No. 8 was fixed at $38 per month. Mr. Lewis Cornelle, principal of No. 6, resigned his position to accept a better offer in the city of Buffalo. He was a thorough, enthusiastic teacher and had the confidence of all his associates, his patrons and pupils. Everyone regretted his determination to leave the city.

In answer to an article published in the *Reveilee* of this city, the following communication signed by a large number of the teachers was read and ordered printed in the above named paper.

" *To the Board of Education,*

" We, the undersigned, teachers in your employ, ask leave, respectfully, to present the following. Having noticed in an article which recently appeared in the Syracuse *Reveilee* over the signature of 'Justice', certain charges against the Clerk of the Board which we believe not only to be inconsistent with the principles of justice, but utterly at variance with the facts, and libellous, we take occasion, therefore, through this medium to offer you the testimony of our experience and observation under his supervision.

" Without wishing in any way to identify ourselves in the discussion now going on before the public, we nevertheless feel constrained, by our love of right and the appreciation of the ability and fidelity of Mr. Salisbury, to testify that we have uniformly found him zealously interested in everything affecting the welfare of our schools and the interests of education ; uniformly free to counsel and encourage. We would also take occasion to express the pleasure and confidence with which we cheerfully coöperate with him in our great common cause."

This was signed by two-thirds of the teachers. At the next meeting of the Board the above communication was received, ordered placed on the records, and the following resolution was unanimously adopted :

" *Resolved,* That in the communication made to this Board by Mr. Salisbury in which reference has necessarily been had to character and qualifications of the teachers of the public schools, he has always manifested a careful regard for their character and interests."

At a meeting held in December, 1849, the following appointments of teachers were made and the salary of each affixed.

No.	1.	G. N. Harris,	$38
	2.	G. N. Taylor,	35
	8.	Edward Smith,	38
	3.	G. D. Reynolds,	40
		Mrs. G. D. Reynolds,	18

No.	3.	Delia N. Earll,	18
		Clara M. Judd,	15
	4.	D. Caverno Allen,	45
		Henrietta White,	18
		Hannah Pomeroy,	15
	9.	Hiram Wyard,	20
	5.	R. R. Stetson,	48
		Mrs. R. R. Stetson,	16
		Jane Vandenburg,	18
		Martha S. Clapp,	18
	6.	Hannah Bennett,	15
	7.	A. G. Salisbury,	60
		Mrs. A. G. Salisbury,	20
		Sarah Wilkinson,	18
		Angelina Butts,	16
		Eliza Williams,	22
		Anna McCombs,	15
	10.	J. B. Brigham,	40
		Frances Larabee,	18
		Almira Barker,	15

Mr. Salisbury having made known his intention to resign his clerkship, his appointment as principal to No. 7 was made before his resignation was made public.

Mr. Salisbury had served as clerk one year, ten months, and during that time had done an immense amount of work in organizing the department. In retiring, Mr. Salisbury read a communication thanking the Board for the support and help he had received from the members, individually and as a body, and for his appointment as principal of No. 7. On motion of Commissioner R. R. Raymond, complimentary resolutions were passed in Mr. Salisbury's behalf.

On January 10, 1850, a ballot for clerk was taken, and Alvan Lathrop was declared elected, but declined the position. On February 1, W. L. Crandall received five votes and was elected clerk, at a salary of $500.

The 2d fiscal year having come to a close, at a meeting held February 18, the Annual Report was read and adopted. An abstract of that report gives the following items :

Total expenditure for 1849, - $10,631.26
Whole number of schools, - - 10
Average number of teachers, - - 25
Number of children between 5 and 16, 4,121
Number of children taught in the schools, 3,121
Average number in daily attendance, 1,266
Increase over last year, - - - 65
Number of children to a teacher, - 51
Number of sittings provided, - 1,460
Number of children on Register, Jan. 1, 1850, 2,193
Excess of registry over accommodations, 733
Number of children in parochial schools, 650
Cost of tuition in private schools, - $19.60
Cost of tuition in public schools, - $5.95
Estimated value of school property, $28,000
Number of volumes in libraries - 3,550

Number of volumes drawn during the year, 7,764

Salaries of principals, from   - $300 to $600

Salaries of assistants, from   - $150 to $220

Accompanying this statistical report was a strong appeal for increased appropriations for providing sittings for all children in the city. The penitentiary had just been built at a cost of $20,000, and the city could and should raise $5,000 this season instead of $1,500, which the charter prescribes, for new buildings and for repairs. Present accommodations would provide for only one-half of the children. Schools by resolution closed one week that teachers might attend the Teachers' Institute.

This closes the records of the 2d year under the new system and a comparison of the statistical tables shows great progress.

The spring election of 1850 made the new Board of Education consist of the following members :

First Ward.—John McCarthy and William II. Hoyt.

Second Ward.—John Wilkinson and Ira A. Thurber.

Third Ward.—Hiram Putnam and R. R. Raymond.

Fourth Ward.—P. C. Samson and Chas. A. Wheaton. Captain Putnam was elected the third time for president.

At a meeting March 21 to consider the appointment of teachers a proposition was again presented for reducing Nos. 1, 2 and 8 to primary schools. The commissioners of the First Ward objected to the change, but

after Mr. Harris was appointed to fill a vacancy in No.
6 school, no objection was made to changing No. 1 to
a primary school.

Mr. Salisbury informed the Board that he could not
consent to remain another year for $600. A committee
was appointed to consult with Mr. Salisbury, the Board
not feeling at liberty to increase his salary, already the
highest paid. After making partial appointments the
Board adjourned for a week when the committee reported that Mr. Salisbury would engage for the first
part of year at the rate of $600, but if longer employed
it must be at the rate of $700. The list of teachers
remained unchanged, except that Mr. Harris was transferred to the principalship of No. 6, as heretofore
mentioned, and Miss Mary Ann Dawson was appointed
teacher in No. 1.

A remonstrance of Mr. McKinstry and others against
longer retaining Mr. Allen in No. 4 was sent to the
Board, and Mr. Allen was asked to respond in writing.
Mr. Brigham, principal of No. 10, also came into dis-
favor, and the patrons sent in a memorial asking for
his removal. Both of these cases were referred for
further investigation. The result was favorable to the
principals.

During the session of the Legislature the city charter
had been so amended that an expenditure of $3,500 a
year was allowed for building purposes, and a discussion came up in the Board as to the advisability of

entering into contract for the expenditure of $7,000, one-half to be paid the first year and the balance the next. This was laid over for further investigation. A committee was appointed to look over the several wards and report the number of new houses needed, and where they should be located.

The difficulty of finding room for all applicants was so great that the Board offered to pay the tuition of all pupils living near the borders if they would attend schools outside the city for a period of four months. The clerk recommended a small increase in the salary of teachers where additional duties had been put upon them or special ability was manifested. He also recommended additional rooms and teachers in the 1st, 3d and 4th Wards ; also that new buildings be erected in three districts by raising the funds available for three years in one year. He further recommended the addition of ten more teachers and an increase in the salary of janitors.

The budget for the current year called for the following items :

For teachers' wages,	$7,923.57
Other current expenses,	1,711.57
To be raised by the city,	7,500.00
From Assessment No. 5, indebtedness at organizaton of the city,	500.00
Assessment on No. 6, same reason,	323.00
For new buildings,	3,500.00

It had been decided that the plan for raising two or three years' appropriation in one year was illegal. After the budget had been agreed upon, Mr. Crandall resigned the position of clerk of the Board of Education, and the first business of the meeting held July, 1850, was the election of a clerk. On the first ballot A. G. Salisbury received five votes, and for the second time was declared clerk of the Board. The competitors for the position were Dr. Stanley of Corning, and L. J. Gillett of this city. A loan of $1,500 for the payment of the teachers was made and the term closed.

J. B. Brigham, on account of the hostility toward him in No. 10 asked that he might be transferred to another school should a vacancy occur. By the resignation of Mr. Salisbury as principal and Miss Butts as assistant in No. 7, two vacancies were to be filled the next term. During the months of August and September the appointments of teachers for the remainder of the school year were completed and were as follows:

			Salary.
No.	1.	Sarah E. Evans,	$20
"	2.	Delia N. Earll,	20
"	3.	George L. Farnham, principal,	50
		Mrs. G. L. Farnham, assistant,	18
		Clara M. Judd, "	18
		Harriet Davis, "	15
"	4.	D. Caverno Allen, principal,	50
		Henrietta B. White, assistant,	20
		Harriet Hull, "	16

No. 5. R. R. Stetson,   principal,   50
        Mrs. R. R. Stetson, assistant,   16
        Elizabeth T. Morgan,   "   20
        Jane A. Vandenburg,   "   18
"   6. G. N. Harris,   principal,   45
        Hannah Burnett,   assistant,   18
"   7. Wm. Van Brocklin,   principal,   50
        Martha S. Clapp,   assistant,   20
        Sarah Wilkinson,   "   20
        Lucy A. Simons,   "   18
        Kate Crawford,   "   16
        Mrs. A. G. Salisbury,   "   22
"   8. Edward Smith,   principal,   40
        Mrs. E. Smith,*   assistant,   16
"   9. Silas Betts,   principal,   30
        Mrs. G. D. Reynolds, assistant,   22
" 10. J. B. Brigham,   principal,   45
        Frances Larabee,   assistant,   18
        Almira Barker,   "   16

A petition, from 39 of the patrons, sent to the Board asking for the removal of Mr. Brigham from the principalship of No. 10, was laid upon the table.

Up to this time the office of the Board had had no permanent abiding place, but meetings had been held in rented rooms where vacant stores and offices could be found at nominal cost. Now convenient, suitable rooms were provided in the north end of the lower floor of the City Hall building.

---

* Resigned during the year, and Aurora Turner became assistant.

A resolution, passed at the September meeting, called for proposals for three new school-houses, one near the old Court House, on North Salina street, one south of No. 7, and one in District No. 9. At a later meeting the proposal for a school-house in District No. 9 was abandoned and the one on the north side was located on Ash street, corner of Townsend ; and the other on Montgomery street, between Adams and Jackson streets. The contracts were signed, and a building committee appointed.

The lots were 8 x 8 and 8 x 9 rods respectively. Both houses were of the same design and were to cost $3,200 each. The one on Ash street was to be completed the 1st of October, and the other in December following.

About this time a petition for the removal of Mr. Allen from the principalship of No. 4 was sent to the Board and the matter was referred to the ward commissioners and the intererested parties for settlement, with the understanding that if they failed to agree, it should be referred to the full Board. The report brought in at the next meeting sustained Mr. Allen and exonerated him.

The adoption of a list of text-books after an investigation of the subjects resulted in the choice of the following list :

Readers.—Webb's Cards, Sanders's Complete Series.

Geography. — Smith's Primary, Mitchell's Quarto, Woodbridge's Higher.

Grammar.—Green's First Lessons, Green's Analysis.

History.—Wilson's United States.

Physiology.—Cutter's Hygiene.

Natural Philosophy.—Perkins's Series.

Astronomy.—Matterson's Bassett.

Arithmetic.—Stoddard's Juvenile (mental), Colburn's First Lessons (mental), Greenleaf's Common School, Greenleaf's National.

Algebra.—Davis's Elementary, Davis's Legendre.

Chemistry.—Silliman's.

Penmanship.—Spencer and Rice's.

Drawing.—Otis's Cards.

Dictionary.—Webster's Quarto and Academic.

This was the first complete list of books adopted by action of the full Board.

No. 5 having become overcrowded, was relieved by fitting up a room in the basement at much less expense than to rent a room and furnish it. Miss Laura A. Huntington was put in charge of it. Mrs. Salisbury of No. 7 and Miss Larabee of No. 10 resigned their positions and their places were filled by the appointment of Charlotte Beebe and Rosetta Pruyn.

Miss Aurora H. Turner of No. 8, having received an appointment to the Albany Normal School, resigned, and her place was filled by the appointment of her sister, Ellen C. Turner.

CHARLES A. WHEATON.

By comparing the third Annual Report with the first we find the number registered 50 less, while the average daily attendance is 258 greater. This, in a marked degree, shows the value of giving close attention to the daily record of each pupil, and to critical, intelligent supervision.

The fourth year of school history under city management began March 15, 1851. After two years of service Commissioner W. H. Hoyt of the First Ward was succeeded by Charles B. Scott, and Commissioner I. A. Thurber of the Second Ward, by J. C. Hanchett. Mr. Hanchett resigned during the year, and Alanson Thorp was appointed in his place. Commissioner Williston from the Third Ward, retired after one and a half years' service, and was followed by Rev. Wm. Bliss Ashley. Commissioner P. C. Samson after two years' service retired from the Board and was followed by Charles A. Wheaton. The president and clerk of the preceding year were unanimously re-elected.

The president stated that Principal Farnham, of No. 3, was inclined to resign, having received a much better offer at Rome, and recommended some action of the Board that his services might be retained in the city. A resolution was passed by which Mr. Farnham was offered $750 for the services of himself and wife for one year, this engagement being on the express condition that they should sign a written contract.

E. A. SHELDON.

Mr. Salisbury again resigned the clerkship, to take effect May 1. E. A. Sheldon and J. B. Brigham were applicants for the position, Mr. Sheldon being successful.

The Onondaga County Institute, which had grown into a strong institution, was given the use of No. 7 for its annual session, ou condition that the rooms should be left in good 'order for the opening of the spring term.

The list of teachers for the term commencing the first of May was essentially the same as at the last appointment, except that Principal Allen of No. 4 had accepted a position at Rome, and Mr. Brigham was transferred to the place. Myron H. Wheaton, a graduate of the Albany State Normal School, was appointed to the principalship of No. 10.

Mr. Allen having asked for a commendatory letter signed by the president and clerk of the Board, a resolution was passed ordering his request to be granted. Some time afterward a note from Mr. Allen appeared in the Syracuse *Standard*, stating that a private and insulting note had been sent to him, but he had not received the one ordered by the Board. At the meeting May 1st, 1851, Mr. Sheldon was asked for an explanation, and said Mr. Allen had made remarks derogatory to the Board of Education, which had caused him to decline to prepare the paper asked for. This explanation was satisfactory and the resolution ordering complimentary statements was rescinded.

We have recorded several complaints from patrons of schools against principals and teachers for various causes and now we record one instituted by a principal against a patron. G. N. Harris, principal of No. 6, made complaint against a Mr. Harrington and son for abusive language and interference with the discipline of the school. The parties were cited to appear before the Board and after a full hearing of the case the following was adopted :

" *Resolved,* That this Board after an impartial examination of the matter between Mr. Harris and Mr. Harrington and son are satisfied that the assault upon Mr. Harris was unprovoked and unjustifiable, and that we do not find anything in the conduct of Mr. Harris to censure.

" *Resolved,* That our confidence in him as a teacher is unimpaired."

Miss H. B. White resigned to accept a better offer, and Miss Harriet Shew was appointed in her place. Miss Emma Brace was also appointed assistant in No. 4, in place of Miss Hull, resigned.

At the June meeting of the Board the building committee reported that the new school building, No. 11, was so far completed that the school had commenced in it, though the outside was not all finished ; and that 180 pupils were in attendance. The transfer of Mr. Betts from No. 9 to No. 11 as principal was approved ;

MR. AND MRS. BETTS.

also the appointment of Miss H. B. White to the principal of No. 9, at a salary of $20 per month.

The first money to be appropriated for supplying books, etc., for any but indigent pupils was set apart at this meeting for the purchase of song books, drawing cards, and Spencer and Rice's copies.

At the meeting in July, 1851, the annual budget was adopted. The clerk asked leave of absence that he might attend the State Teachers' Association at Buffalo, August 6 and 7, and that the next monthly meeting be held August 9.

A special meeting for the appointment of teachers was held August 11, and resulted in renewing the appointments made in May, with slight changes made necessary by opening No. 12, to which Edward Smith was removed as principal and the Misses H. B. and her sister Louise White were appointed assistants. At a later meeting, Galen Wilson was appointed principal of No. 8, from which Mr. Smith had been transferred.

No. 12 was in a district, even at that time, comprised largely of Germans, and it was natural that parents should desire to have their children instructed in their native tongue. A petition was presented asking for a German teacher. While they did not immediately secure this, we shall see that at a later day they succeeded.

After ordering a loan of $2,900 for the payment of teachers in anticipation of the collection of the city taxes, and ordering that the summer vacation occupy four weeks, the fall term to commence September 15, the Board adjourned.

It will be noticed that teachers did not receive pay for their services except at the end of the term, and in some instances then only in orders on the city treasurer, to be paid when the taxes were collected. Many of those engaged in teaching were obliged to get trusted for board, clothing and other necessaries, with the understanding of the creditors that they would be paid at the close of the term. Such promises could only be kept by getting these orders cashed less the discount. Many of the employees suffered not only from small compensation, but from loss in buying on time with the further loss of deductions for interest. The Board were not to blame for this. They depended upon the city for the means to carry on the schools ; taxes were not paid till late in the fall or winter, while contracts were made early in the season. Thus without means at the command of the city except by making loans, the Common Council preferred to allow employees to wait for tax collection. I suppose this was true in all departments of the city government.

As has been previously stated, No. 9 was situated on West street. The lot was small, being 50 x 100 feet. In September of this year this lot was exchanged by a payment of $50, for a lot on Seymour street, 8 rods square. This lot was afterward increased by purchasing a slip from the Trinity Church Society, making a lot of 10 rods frontage.

During the summer vacation, Principal R. R. Stetson was suddenly removed by death. His funeral was held in the old Congregational church, on East Genesee street, on ground occupied by Convention Hall for many years. The funeral was attended by a large number of teachers and others interested in education. Mr. Stetson was a thorough instructor, of kind impulses and generous heart. He was a strict disciplinarian, some thought severe. Some of his old pupils can testify to his agility and strength, when with his one arm he would throw the delinquent across his knee and apply the ruler with repeated and well-directed blows not soon to be forgotten. Notwithstanding these not often recurring scenes he was beloved and honored by his pupils. The Board passed the following :

" *Resolved,* That, in the death of Mr. Stetson, the Board of Education and the cause have lost an able, efficient teacher : one whose entire energies were devoted to the cause in which he labored.

" *Resolved,* That the clerk be desired to enter these resolutions upon the records, and transmit a copy to Mrs. Stetson, with the respectful assurance of our sympathy and condolence with her in this hour of bereavement."

Mr. C. O. Roundy was appointed to the principalship of No. 5 to succeed Mr. Stetson.

CHARLES O. ROUNDY.

An addition was made to the lot of No. 3 of 4 x 11 rods, at a cost of $600.

All children using pen and ink were required to purchase sets of copies provided by the Board, and teachers were forbidden to set copies. This was regarded by some of the pupils and patrons as an arbitrary enactment. Teachers however considered it a great relief, for it was not an easy task for one to make from 50 to 100 pens from goose quills, some of which were not of the best, and to write the same number of copies between the close of school and before time for commencing the next morning session. It must be remembered this was before the steel pen had come into use.

In February, 1852, Mr. Betts's salary was raised to $50 per month. The Annual Report of the Clerk, E. A. Sheldon, was sent to the Common Council, with the request that it be published in pamphlet form. This was the 4th Annual Report, and the first one so published.

All lower grades were overcrowded, notwithstanding the increased facilities added during the year. The year closed with better classification and grading, more complete courses of study, a better system of penmanship, the introduction of music, the holding of weekly teachers' meetings, a more perfect settlement of district boundaries, and the discouragement of corporal punishment.

A plea for a high school was strongly presented, and one was greatly needed to complete the school system. Four years had passed and no definite action had been taken towards accomplishing this much desired object.

At the last meeting in this fiscal year, February 25, 1852, Mr. Farnham's salary was increased to $70 per month, and Mrs. Farnham's to $20, in order to retain their services, as he had been offered a position at Buffalo at $750 a year. Greater advancements in all departments of school work had been made during this than during any preceding year since the city organization.

March 4, 1852, at its final meeting, the old Board recommended the opening of two evening schools the coming year for the benefit of such young persons as are compelled to work during the day. The retiring commissioners were, John McCarthy from the First Ward, John Wilkinson from the Second Ward, and Hiram Putnam from the Third Ward. Captain Putnam had also served as president of the Board since its organization. In his remarks in closing his work as a commissioner, Captain Putnam said the schools were never in so good condition and everything looked promising for the future interests of this department of city work. He urged thorough and vigorous watchfulness on the part of those who were to have the future responsibility of this important trust, and pledged that his utmost efforts should be added. A hearty, earnest and sincere vote of thanks was tendered to him.

The new Board immediately convened. The new commissioners were James Lynch of the First Ward, John B. Burnett of the Second Ward, and Lewis J. Gillett of the Third Ward. Captain Putnam was invited to sit with the new Board.

Charles A. Wheaton was elected president, and Mr. Sheldon was re-elected clerk, at a salary of $700.

At a meeting held April 5, the fiscal and school years were both made to begin January 1, and end with December. This rule did not stand long, for the State school year at that time began October 1. This made it necessary for two annual school reports each year.

It was at this meeting that the project of establishing a central library originated, and a committee was appointed to recommend a plan. A report was made combining all the district libraries into one, to be called the Central Library. Commissioner Lynch asked that the First Ward be exempted from this combination, on account of the great distance children and older citizens would have to go to get the benefit to be derived from the library. Branches of the Central Library were established at School No. 3 in the Fifth Ward, in Lodi school, and in the City Hall building.

At a meeting held April 23, Mrs. Farnham from No. 3, and Myron Wheaton from No. 10, resigned their positions. Mr. Wheaton's resignation was afterward withdrawn. Miss Maria Isham was transferred from No. 4 to Mrs. Farnham's place.

A contract was given to A. L. Mason for enlarging No. 8 and building a new house in District No. 9, conditioned on his accepting $3,500 during the current year and the remainder the next year.

The office of the Board was put in better condition and new book-cases were ordered for the Central Library.

A committee which had been appointed to consider the subjects of absence and tardiness made the following report :

"Any pupil who shall have been absent to the amount of three school days in any term, except by reason of sickness, sickness in the family, or absence from the city, shall not be entitled to continue or be admitted to any other school until duly restored by the ward commissioner ; and three cases of tardiness shall be equivalent to one absence and treated as such."

This was incorporated into the rules of the Board and has remained with slight changes to the present time.

Mr. Farnham was again offered inducements to leave the city, this time to take charge of a female seminary in Indianapolis, and he accepted the offer, though it called out a protest from citizens in his district and a request to the Board not to allow any pecuniary consideration to stand in the way of retaining him.   August 23, the committee on teachers reported for appointment M. L. Brown principal of No. 3, and W. L. Cook principal of No. 9, with a few other unimportant changes

M. L. Brown.

of the teachers.   Soon after his appointment, Mr.
Brown sent a letter saying that his engagements at
Corning were such that he could not accept the position until the middle of October, but should a vacancy
then exist, he would gladly accept it.   John Stacy was
appointed temporarily.

A newspaper in the city had assailed Mr. Sheldon in
his position as clerk, and Commissioner Gillett in a
Board meeting offered the following:

"WHEREAS, complaints have been made through
some of the city papers against the clerk of this Board,
and which tends, indirectly to the discredit of this body,
therefore be it

"*Resolved*, That the clerk has our entire confidence
and we recommend him not to answer any more com-
munications of that description."

A request coming from the pupils of No. 5 that they
might be excused from school at 3 o'clock, P.M., was
denied.

December 2, 1852, the committee on revision of rules
reported the following amendments : That the school
year shall consist of 44 weeks, and shall be divided into
three terms, the first commencing the first week in
January and the beginning and length of each successive term to be determined by the Board at the close
of the preceding term.

Two evening schools were opened, one in the First
Ward in charge of Truman van Tassel, and the other

in the central part under Mr. Harris. This was the first attempt to establish evening schools.

January 6, 1853, the reports of committees on revision of rules and to consider the propriety of establishing a high school were considered and discussed, and both reports were adopted and ordered printed in pamphlet form. This was the second printed report, and was much more complete than the preceding one.

At a special meeting appointed to hear Q. A. Johnson on the regulations governing attendance and tardiness of children and in support of a complaint made by three of the patrons against teachers who, in conformity to the rule, had kept children from school on account of repeated absences, Mr. Johnson raised objection against the spirit and operation of the rule. He spoke at length on the powers of the Board and against the legality, utility and public policy of the regulation. After considerable discussion a resolution to refer this rule to a committee, resulted in the following, which was adopted :

" Any pupil who shall have been absent from school to the amount of three full days, not certified as necessary, shall be required to produce the certificate of his parent or guardian (which may be verbal, if delivered by the parent or guardian in person), that such absence was necessary or unavoidable, with or without the knowledge or consent (as the case may be) of such parent or guardian ; and in case the parent or guardian shall neglect or refuse to give such certificate, then the pupil shall be suspended until such certificate shall be given. Three cases of tardiness shall be equivalent to an absence and shall be treated as such."

The annual report contained the usual items. No. 8 had been enlarged by adding 16 feet to the length and raising the whole to make a two-story building, giving a seating capacity of nearly 200 pupils. It was still too small. A new school-house had been built in District No. 9.

The annual meeting for 1853 was held March 8. The Board received for new commissioners Matthew Murphy from the First Ward, Q. A. Johnson from the Second Ward, and William Hall from the Third Ward. The president and clerk were re-elected. The principals appointed were unchanged, except the appointment of James Johonnot to No. 4, in place of Mr. Brigham, retired. Among the new teachers were the Misses C. A. Rose and Mary Earll in No. 3, Donna Evans in No. 4, Martha Weaver and Henrietta Leonard in No 5, and Mary Slocum in No. 7.

At the May meeting, Mr. Sheldon resigned the office of clerk to accept a like position in the city of Oswego, which he considered a more promising field. Mr. Sheldon had occupied the position two years to the entire satisfaction of the Board, the teachers and the community. After a long service in the city of Oswego as superintendent of schools, he was appointed to the principalship of the Oswego State Normal School, where he still remains as one of the prominent leading educational men of the State of York. The Oswego Normal School has had a decided influence on educational thought throughout the country, and its graduates are universally in demand as among the best in the field. Commissioner William Hall was appointed to fill the position made vacant by the resignation of Mr. Sheldon, and continued until March 21, 1854.

The annual budget asked of the Common Council was $15,140.42. The beginning of the fall term was fixed for September 6. The salaries of the principals of No. 8 and 9 were made equal to that of other men principals. On September 6, James Johonnot resigned the principalship of No. 4, and Perez Brown was appointed to succeed him. On September 23, another addition was ordered to be put upon the N. W. corner of No. 8, two stories high, large enough for two rooms.

At the October meeting, Commissioner Gillett of the Third Ward resigned, and the Common Council appointed Ansel E. Kinne to succeed him till the end of the year. Evening schools were conducted in Nos. 3, 5 and 7 under the charge of the principals of these schools.

The new Board organized March 21 with an increase in the membership to sixteen, the city being now divided into eight wards instead of four, with two commissioners from each.

ANSEL E. KINNE.

The members were as follows :

First Ward.—John McCarthy, Wm. F. Gere.

Second Ward.—Walter C. Hopkins, Matthew Murphy.

Third Ward.—P. S. Stoddard, Q. A. Johnson.

Fourth Ward.—N. F. Graves, J. G. Wynkoop.

Fifth Ward.—H. L. Dinmore, A. E. Kinne.

Sixth Ward.—Wm. Bliss Ashley, Wm. Hall.

Seventh Ward.—H. D. Hatch, E. T. Hayden.

Eighth Ward.—W. H. H. Smith, George Barney.

N. F. Graves was elected president, and M. L. Brown, principal of No. 3, was elected clerk.

Another effort was made April 18, to reduce Nos. 4, 8, and 11 to intermediate schools, which resulted in a vote to carry out the proposition in No. 11 on condition that the present teachers be continued on the pay-roll for the year. On December 12, the proposition was renewed as to No. 4, and succeeded. The changes were made to curtail expenses in the school department and secure better grading.

A loan was made at this meeting for the payment of the teachers, janitors and for cleaning. Quite a percentage of the indebtedness to teachers had been included in the funded debt of the city.

One of the city papers offered to print the proceedings of the Board provided the clerk would put them in suitable form, and consent was given on condition that it be done without expense to the Board.

On August 1, the teachers were appointed for the next term, to open September 1. There were few changes, but Misses Corbin and Anderson were added.

December 19, Wm. H. Cook resigned the principalship of No. 3 and a petition of over 200 names was presented to the Board asking for the appointment of Edward Smith to the position. Another petition was presented from District No. 8 asking that no change be made in principalship of that school. The matter was laid on the table for further consideration as was also the proposition for organizing a high school.

In December a committee reported a plan for a high school to occupy temporarily the upper floor of schoolhouse No. 5, with C. O. Roundy principal, assisted by Perez Brown. On January 1, 1855, Daniel Losey, a graduate of the Albany Normal School, was made principal of No. 3, A. E. Kinne, principal of No. 5, and Edward Smith, principal of No. 8. Syracuse was thus among the first cities of the State to establish a high school.

On January 16, at a special meeting to provide for overcrowded schools, the Board appointed the Misses Jane Porter and Sarah Wagner to fill vacancies in No. 5, rented W. J. Blair's store, and placed Miss Burnham there to give additional relief for that school. A chapel was rented on Church street (now West Willow), and Mrs. Lewis appointed teacher to relieve No. 4. A new room was opened in No. 8 and a teacher appointed.

Daniel Losey.

All admissions to the High School were referred to the teachers' committee and the clerk, and a resolution was passed requiring an examination for all applicants for positions as teachers. A committee had been appointed to prepare suitable provision for further revision to the city charter.

February 19, 1855, two extra rooms were prepared for No. 7 and one for No. 9, and the principals were asked to report to the Board all non-resident pupils now in attendance in the schools. The retiring members were W. F. Gere, First Ward, W. C. Hopkins, Second Ward, Q. A. Johnson, Third Ward, J. G. Wynkoop, Fourth Ward, G. H. Hulin, Fifth Ward ; Commissioners Dinmore, Kinne and Hayden had resigned during the year.

The new Board met March 20, 1855. N. F. Graves was re-elected president, and George L. Farnham was elected clerk at a salary of $800, his appointment to take effect May 1. M. L. Brown had decided to remove to Auburn and start a young ladies' seminary. He proved himself as popular and successful there as he had been here, always respected by his patrons and loved by his pupils.

The annual report of the last Board was ordered printed in pamphlet form, with an edition of 500 copies.

An effort to secure better accommodation for the High school resulted in its transfer from No. 5 to the upper floor of School No. 4. Announcement was

made that an examination of teachers would take place
April 30. All teachers were asked to be present except
those holding certificates issued by the State Department or the normal school; and these were invited to
take the examination. There were present 22 women
teachers and 3 men, who were reported to be entitled
to certificates, while 17 of the old teachers not holding
State certificates and 4 women who did hold such certificates had also tried the examination and deserved
commendation for the courage they had shown and the
success of their efforts. The committee further
reported the appointment of 54 teachers, the principals
remaining the same as last term.

District No. 12 had made repeated application for a
male principal since the transfer of Mr. Smith, and F.
A. Loomis was put in charge at a salary of $60 per
month. Mrs. Hewes, the former principal received a
vote of thanks from the Board for excellent work in
the school under her charge and an expression of undi-
minished confidence in her as a teacher and instructor.

By reason of a general complaint of overcrowded
rooms in the primary department, the Board passed a
resolution instructing teachers to admit no more pupils
than could be comfortably provided with seats. First
applicants were to have the preference, but if pupils
became irregular in attendance their seats might be
given to other pupils desiring admission. A request
was sent to the Common Council strongly urging them
to provide greater accommodations.

The breaking out of the small pox in the Second Ward caused considerable excitement in the city and No. 12, being in the immediate vicinity, was ordered closed by the Board of Health.

During the month of August an examination of pupils was made for admission to the High school. Perez Brown resigned his position as teacher, and Rev. R. R. Raymond was appointed assistant principal.

At the November meeting, the Board requested teachers to report the best methods of primary teaching, and also to record in a book provided for that purpose all cases of corporal punishment inflicted in their several schools, with the date, cause of punishment, how inflicted and the result—the same to be open for the inspection of any member of the Board. This was the strongest effort against the use of the rod that had ever been made in this city. The evil was diminished but not eradicated till a decade later.

During the month of December great complaints were made against the furnaces in No. 9 school-house. Both winters the house had been occupied, teachers and pupils had suffered from the cold, and on extremely cold days the school was closed. After resorting to every known means of remedying the evil, the furnaces were abandoned and stoves were put in.

No. 4 school-house was found to be inadequate to the wants of the High school and a movement for providing a better place resulted in securing rooms in the

Pike block, 3d floor, entrance on West Fayette street, to be fitted up by the Board at an expense of $400. The lease was to continue five years at $450, with the privilege of five years more at the same rate. The tuition of non-resident pupils of this school was fixed at $4 per term for higher English and $5 for languages. On account of failing health, Mr. Roundy, at his request, was granted a leave of absence; and the clerk, Mr. Farnham, was requested to take charge of his classes during that term.

Misses Donna Evans and Delia N. Earll resigned their positions as teachers, both of them to go to California where they could secure better pay in a better climate. Letters highly commendatory from the Board introduced them to school authorities wherever they should choose to locate. Miss Earll had been in the schools of what is now the First Ward one or two years before the city organization, and possessed more than common ability.

Resolutions of regret were passed that Commissioners McCarthy, Freeoff, Stoddard, Graves, Ashley, Hatch and Smith were to retire from the Board with the acknowledgments of their acceptable work during the past year. Similar resolutions commendatory of the president and clerk were recorded.

The new Board met March 18, 1856. Commissioner LeRoy Morgan was elected president and George L. Farnham was re-elected clerk. The budget was read and adopted and a resolution prevailed asking the Common Council to give $17,000, the whole amount asked, and in addition the sum of $5,000 for a permanent fund. The request was granted. On account of inadequate accommodations a resolution was passed denying the privilege to attend the public schools to any who do not draw public money.

The property known as the " Hemlock Church " was purchased for $900, thereby relieving the schools in the Fourth, Seventh, and Eighth Wards.

Commissioner Johnson introduced a resolution forbidding the teaching of the languages in the public schools during the regular school hours. Although the High school had been opposed by taxpayers and by educated and intelligent men, in the Board and out of it, on the ground of injustice in taxing the people for higher education, Mr. Johnson was the first, and the only one, in the Board of Education to antagonize that institution publicly.

D. F. Brown of Auburn presented to the teachers at one of their meetings a beautiful piece of pen-work entitled "'The Lord's Prayer " for inspection, and made application to the Board for the use of a room in one of the school buildings for teaching penmanship to such as would like to avail themselves of the opportunity. The request was granted, and many of the teachers entered the class.

On May 5, Mr. Roundy sent a communication resigning the principalship of the High school, saying he could not afford to remain, much as he loved the work and the pupils under his care. Three positions had been offered him at an advance upon the salary he was receiving here. His salary was increased to $1,000, which called out a request from the other teachers for an increase. On May 20, the salary of the clerk was fixed at $1,000.

Up to this time nothing better than pineboard desks and seats with common paint had been furnished the best of the school-houses, but in fitting up the High school, desks made of cherry with chairs to match, known as Boston school furniture, were provided.

Charles E. Fitch who resided and was educated here for college and had just graduated from Williams was appointed July 1, to assist in the High school four days in the week, at $1 per day. In August, Miss Kate Pool was appointed assistant in No. 9 at $20 per month. She remained in the employment of the Board a quarter of a century, when she married Mr. Baldwin, but within two or three years was left a widow. Miss Pool was one of the best primary teachers in the city.

It was not uncommon for the Board to find itself in financial embarassment, with no means of paying bills or salaries, and a resolution was passed to close school till such time as the Common Council should provide funds. It was afterward reconsidered and laid on the

table, but secured the desired aid. The Board asked
the Common Council to sell a vacant lot on Onondaga
street, and apply $1,000 from the sale in building a
school-house on the lot lately purchased on Fayette
street, and to use the remainder in repairing No. 7
school-house. Late in the autumn the three evening
schools were opened.

On December 5, 1856, a special meeting of the Board
was called to take action relating to the death of one of
its members, Commissioner Q. A. Johnson. A committee on resolutions was appointed and the following was
presented and adopted :

"This Board having heard with regret of the death
of Q. A. Johnson, Esq., a respected and worthy member of this Board, therefore,

" *Resolved*, That we deeply sympathize with the family and friends of the deceased, and that as a mark of
respect we will attend his funeral in a body to-morrow
afternoon at 3 o'clock.

" *Resolved*, That a copy of this resolution be sent to
the family of the deceased."

In January, 1857, a successful effort was made to
secure the $500 apportionment to cities employing a
superintendent of schools.

Edward Smith resigned the principalship of No. 8
with the expectation of engaging in farming. At the
meeting in February Henry A. Barnum (afterward Gen.
Barnum), was appointed to the position vacated. After

EDWARD SMITH.

a little time Mr. Smith returned to the city and took charge of the ungraded winter school in the First Ward. In the spring of 1860, Principal Wheaton being compelled by sickness to leave school for several weeks, Mr. Smith filled that position until he was able to return. On account of failing health Mr. Losey, principal of No. 3, was obliged to retire from teaching and Mr. Smith became his successor.

An amendment to the city charter required'the election of one commissioner in each ward instead of two, as heretofore, the commissioners to hold office for two years, one-half to be elected on alternate years, the even wards in one year and the odd ones on the following year. This did not meet with favor from the Board and a protest was vigorously made, but without effect. It is presumed that even the objectors became fully satisfied with the change after trial, for small bodies generally work together with less friction than larger ones.

The new Board elected Wm. J. Hough, president and George L. Farnham clerk, at a salary of $1,000. Joseph C. Calanen, Esq., who was elected from the Third Ward, died before its organization, and W. V. Bruyn was appointed.

In April of this year measures were taken for the enlargement of No. 5 by the addition of a wing extending toward the west, two stories in height. This was completed at a cost of $2,053. Another room in

No. 9 was finished off for the opening of the next term. On April 24, R. F. Stevens took his place in the Board, having been appointed in place of Mr. Williamson who had resigned.

At the May meeting a resolution was passed authorizing the president and clerk to draw orders monthly instead of at the end of the term for the payment of teachers and others in the regular employ of the Board. This was the beginning of the monthly payment of fixed salaries which has since continued.

In June, blanks to be filled out by teachers informing parents of absences and tardiness of their children, were adopted, with the hope that these evils might be mitigated and the schools thereby benefitted. This had the desired effect as was shown by the monthly reports.

The schoolhouse on Fayette street (now called Irving school), had been so nearly completed that a room was finished off, and the school opened under Miss Louise Moss,—transferred from No. 7. This afforded some relief to No. 7. During this summer the Board concluded to give the contract for the enlargement of No. 7 to some responsible party on condition that payments should be made no faster than funds had been provided for that purpose.

I believe that this was the first year that all schools were to be heated with coal, and the amount needed was purchased at $5.50 per ton.

Misses Mahala G. Hall, Harriet N. Brand and Maria Burke were appointed assistants in No. 7. In September, Mr. Betts resigned the principalship, and A. G. Salisbury was again appointed to that position, at a salary of $800. After Mr. Salisbury's resignation from No. 7 he had opened a private school in the Myers Block, which he made popular and successful. The rooms were provided with the best furniture and apparatus. It seemed desirable to the Board to secure Mr. Salisbury's services in the public schools because he was a popular and successful teacher, and his influence would draw pupils from the private into the public schools. Having established the practice of equal salaries to principals it would not be practicable to pay him more than others were receiving and the plan adopted was to employ Mrs. Salisbury as assistant at $350, then a large salary, and purchase the furniture, etc., used in the private school, at a cost of $356.75.

Miss Sylvia J. Eastman was appointed assistant in No. 7. She afterward went to Buffalo and for a number of years was preceptress of the High school there at a large salary.

During the autumn of this year at the suggestion of Commissioner Allen $15 was appropriated to purchase a number of books on the phonetic method for the purpose of testing it. After trial in one school with results likely to prove beneficial it was adopted in all the primary departments, and for a time gave Syracuse schools considerable notoriety. It was used for a number of years, and though considerably modified has never been abandoned. The phonetic system was changed in 1866 to the phonic, essentially the same except that in the latter the common alphabet is used.

The meetings of the teachers since the first had been on every Monday evening, but now they became semi-monthly, on Saturday mornings from 9 to 12. This change was made because of the inconvenience to the ladies of getting to the place of meeting at night. There were no means of public conveyance, streets and walks were often muddy, or, in winter, blocked by deep snows, streets were not well lighted, and distances from the outlying districts were long.

At the November meeting Miss Mary J. Hopkins, who had just graduated from the High school, was appointed assistant in the senior department of No. 7. She was afterward transferred to the Salina school and put in charge of the junior department, where she remained two or three years. During this time she was married to A. D. Perry, a business man of this city. She was afterward made assistant in the High school, where she remained until her death in 1882. Mrs. Perry was a teacher of peculiar power and influence over the young. She was greatly beloved and honored by her pupils, and there are many now living who remember her with esteem and veneration.

Mr. Roundy asked for leave of absence on account of

failing health and Mr. Long was appointed to his place temporarily. When the committee visited the school they found him in poor health, and closed the school for two weeks, till Mr. Roundy was able to return.

Col. George, chief of the Onondaga tribe of Indians, sent a petition to the Board asking the privilege of sending his son into one of the public schools of the city free of charge. The request was granted and the boy remained in No. 7 for several months under the supervision of Mrs. Salisbury, making considerable progress.

Up to this time the records of the several schools combined did not show the actual number of pupils in the schools, and a plan was adopted to prevent duplicate registrations by requiring teachers to record the names of pupils who had been registered in other schools only upon their presenting a transfer from the school which they had attended, setting forth the number of days they had been present, the number of days of absence, the number of times tardy, the amount of time lost by tardiness, the grade in the school, and the reason of the transfer. After being registered in the new school and notice having been given of this fact to the principal where the pupil had been previously registered, his name and record were cancelled. The rules and regulations were revised and 500 copies were printed for distribution.

This fiscal year closed March 12, 1858 at which time four commissioners from the odd wards retired from the Board by limitation of the revised charter.

CHAPTER III

SECOND DECADE—1858 TO 1867

The new provision for one commissioner from each ward now came fully into effect and the body consisted of the following, in the order of the wards : N. M. Childs, Charles M. Henderson, Wm. V. Bruyn, J. J. Peck, W. W. Willard, Richard F. Stevens, Joseph A. Allen and Charles L. Chandler.

N. M. Childs was elected president and Mr. Farnham was unanimously elected clerk.

The budget for the current year was adopted and by a committee presented to the city council. A collection of the books of reference and of books not read by children in the district libraries was concentrated at the Central Library, thereby taking the second step toward a single library for the city.

The increase of pupils in several of the schools called for extra accommodations, and one room in the new addition to No. 7 was furnished, the upper story of No. 13 was finished off, and both were enclosed by a substantial and ornamental fence. Mrs. A. E. Kinne resigned her position as principal of the primary department of No. 5.

Fifty-six teachers were appointed at the beginning of the school year and several more were added during the fall term.

An additional room in the City Hall was secured by the Board of Education for the better accommodation of the Central Library, which had now become an established institution, and James Strachan became the first librarian and assistant to the superintendent, at a salary of $300.

Mrs. Farnham on account of her health asked leave of absence. This was allowed, and Miss Eastman was given the position temporarily, and afterward appointed to it permanently, for after a few weeks Mrs. Farnham died. At the meeting in November the Board passed resolutions of condolence and sympathy which were entered upon the records.

Miss Caroline Lounsbury was appointed assistant in No. 4. She remained connected with the same school until 1873, when she resigned to go to California where she engaged in teaching and after a while married. In September Miss Ellen M. Swain entered the High school as an additional assistant. Miss Swain was finely educated, a lady in her deportment and association with her pupils, and an excellent teacher. While she continued she made her influence reach every pupil

SAMUEL J. MAY.

in the school. Ellen M. Cheney entered No. 9 this year. She passed through several grades and was finally made assistant to the principal. She continued in this position for several years and resigned because of illness. She never resumed her work, except for short intervals to supply temporary vacancies.

Mary Burke was another teacher who began her services this year I think in No. 12, but soon was transferred to No. 7, where she remained most of the time principal of the primary department till the Adams school on Adams street was opened in 1874. She was appointed as its first principal. After 24 years of service she resigned, being worn and sick ; and the next year, after much suffering she passed away. She was a notable primary teacher. Miss Carrie Morris succeeded Miss Moss as principal of No. 13.

Rev. S. J. May donated 22 volumes to the Central Library which were gratefully accepted, and a special place was set apart in the reading room for the books. In November of this year the First Ward winter ungraded school was opened under charge of Edward Smith. It will be recollected that Mr. Smith resigned his position in No. 8 in the spring of 1857, and at request of Mr. Farnham, he returned to take charge of this school. An evening school in No. 7 was opened the same winter.

During the winter following a course of free lectures in the City Hall was given under the auspices of the Board of Education. The lecturers were all residents

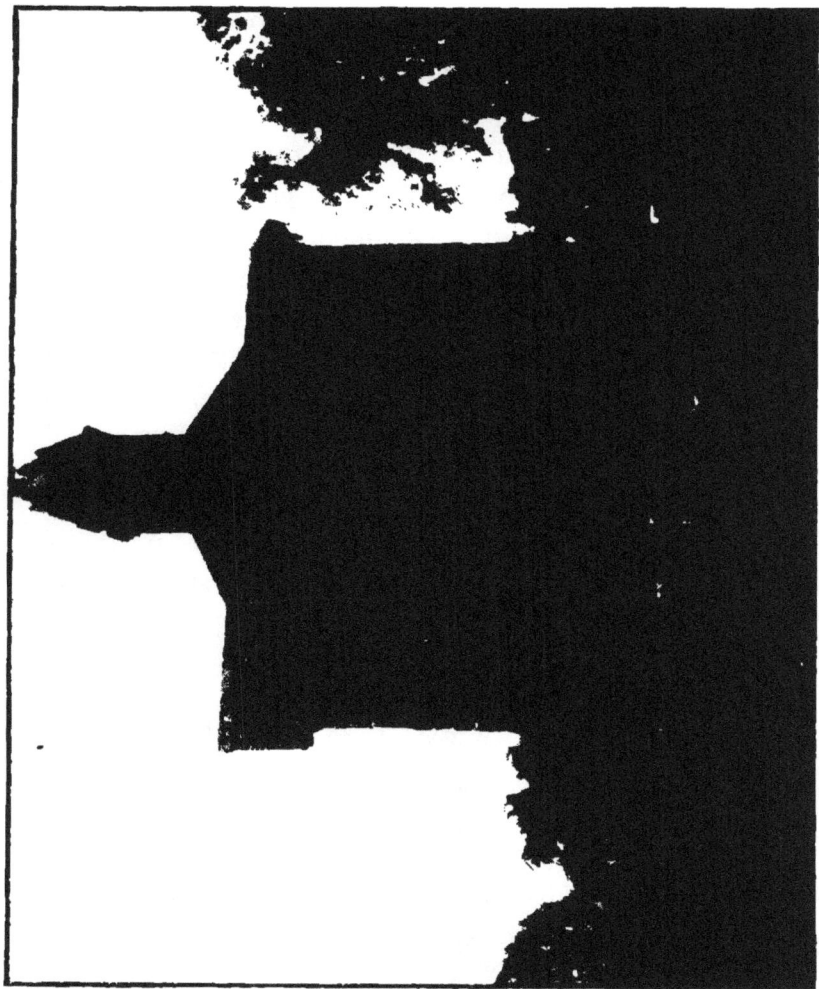

SALINA SCHOOL.

of the city,—Hon. Charles B. Sedgwick, Rev. I. O.
Filmore, Hon. Dennis McCarthy, Rev. J. M. Clark,
Charles E. Fitch, and J. G. K. Truair. The course
was well attended, entertaining and profitable.

In February, 1859, the Common Council authorized
the sale of Nos. 1, 2 and 8 and the purchase of what
was known as the Richmond property in the First
Ward. The plan was carried out and the lot named
was purchased for $2,400. During that year and the
following spring the house now known as Salina school
was built.

The Franklin Institute, having been organized some
time before, gave a public display of its collections,
natural and historical, to which the school chidren were
invited as a means
of education.

Gen. J. J. Peck.

At the organiza-
tion of the new
Board, March 22,
1859, J. J. Peck was
elected president,
and G. L. Farn-
ham, clerk and su-
perintendent of
schools. The title
of superintendent
of schools had been
added to that of
clerk of the Board

when application was made to the State department for the $500 appropriated to cities where the schools were under the general direction of a city superintendent.

After the close of the winter school in the First Ward, Mr. Smith was put into No. 10 as a supply in place of Mr. Wheaton, where he remained until Mr. Wheaton returned. Mr. Wheaton however on April 10 sent in his resignation. He was a graduate of the Albany Normal school, one of the first after its organization. He was a popular and successful teacher, and the district, his associate teachers, and the Board all acknowledged his worth. Upon his vacating the position the school was made a junior and primary one and Miss Orra M. Gaylord was appointed principal.

Plans having been matured for a new building in the First Ward an arrangement was also made to build another in the Fourth Ward. A contract was entered into with A. L. Mason for the sums $9,706 and $3,800 respectively, the buildings to be completed, one in October, 1859, and the other in May, 1860.

The lot selected in the Fourth Ward was on the east side of Lodi street on the side of a quite a steep hill. The commissioner of that ward had the credit of the selection and congratulated himself for securing so beautiful and excellent a situation for a school. It has proved to be anything but what he expected. The drainage from a large part of the yard goes under and around the building, it is slippery and dangerous in winter, and is more expensive to keep in repair than a level lot would be.

Up to this time all school libraries in districts not included in the Central Library had been controlled by the local authorities and the Central by the Board of Education, but now all of them came under the Central control.

Children were allowed to draw books but once a week not including those in the primary grades. At the July meeting of the Board the designation of schools by numbers was discontinued and names substituted.

Hereafter Nos. 1, 2, and 8 were dropped and Salina school represents them.

No. 3 is now known as Jefferson school.

No. 4 is now known as Genesee school.

No. 5 is now known as Prescott school.

No. 6 was known as Fayette school. Now abandoned.

No. 7 is now known as Putnam school.

No. 9 is now known as Seymour school.

No. 10 was known as Lodi school. Now abandoned and Madison school takes its place.

No. 11 is now known as Montgomery school.

No. 12 is now known as Townsend school.

No. 13 is now known as Irving school.

The new school on Lodi street was named Clinton school.

LODI SCHOOL.

The Hebrews sent in a petition asking to have their children dismissed at half past three that they might study their own language, and another asking for the use of a room in Putnam school (No. 7) for a debating club. Both were denied. Another free lecture course was opened for the fall and winter, Hon. T. T. Davis, Rev. S. J. May, and others appearing.

During the spring of 1860, Mr. Losey, principal of Jefferson school (No. 3), on account of ill-health was obliged to give up teaching for a while, and Edward Smith, who was teaching the winter school, at request of the superintendent, closed the school (it being reduced in numbers), and supplied in Mr. Losey's place. Later in the season, on the resignation of Mr. Losey, Mr. Smith was appointed principal of Jefferson school. After a long service, which had been eminently successful, the Board and the patrons of Jefferson school parted with the services of Principal Losey with regret, and there stands by vote of the Board most complimentary records of his worth as a teacher and citizen.

During the early spring the teachers and pupils of the High school gave an entertainment, the proceeds of which were applied to the purchase of a piano for the school. It was a success, as similar school exercises have proved to be.

The new Board organized with all the old commissioners except the one from the Second Ward, which was filled by Commissioner Jacob Miller. The president and clerk and superintendent were re-elected. In April a committee from the Onondaga County Asylum asked for some arrangement with the Board by which the school connected with that institution could receive the benefits of city supervision. A committee from the two bodies in conference agreed that the Asylum should provide school room to accommodate 100 pupils and all necessary appliances, and the Board of Education should provide text-books and teachers.

At the request of the German population of the Second Ward, a German assistant was appointed to teach that language in Townsend school.

The examinations of the schools were made through marked books so that all pupils of similar grades had the same questions. This resulted in showing better results than any preceding trial.

In the examination for candidates for teachers only the graduates of the High school, and particularly those who had been in the teachers' class organized under the Board of Regents of the University, were admitted. From this date the majority of applicants for teaching have been graduates of the High school.

The Salina school was completed in May and dedicatory exercises were held at the building under direction of the Board and Principal Smith. The president took charge of the senior room, and introduced Rev. S. J. May, who gave the principal address, afterward printed in full in the annual report for 1861. Other speakers followed, including the president, the superintendent of schools, and Dr. H. D. Didama. The singing was under the lead of Miss Hattie Abbott, and a collation for all who attended the exercises was provided by teachers and pupils. The school had seats for 600 pupils, and was the largest that had been erected since the city organization.

The whole number of teachers at the beginning of this 12th year under city care was three times the number appointed in 1848. The new York State Teachers' Association in June of this year was by a unanimous vote invited to hold its session here. Our citizens opened their doors to all lady teachers free of charge. A large attendance assembled in Wieting Hall for an uncommonly wide-awake and stirring session. Susan B. Anthony was among the number that gave life and spirit to the daily gatherings. Miss Anthony advocated woman's rights in every department of human industry, and was as vigorously opposed by her namesake Principal Anthony of Albany. Although at times almost turbulent from the excitement of debate the president, by his genial manner and perfect self-control, while allowing each his fair privilege, was able to preserve good order and conduct each discussion to a just conclusion.

A lot for a new school-house in the Third Ward, opposite the present High school, was purchased for $3,000. This was then a low-sunken hole, but it was

GENESEE SCHOOL.

partially filled in, and is still used as Genesee school, though it has never been brought up to grade.

Two extra teachers were needed but from lack of funds they were not appointed. Mrs. Perry was transferred from Salina to the High school. Commissioner Joseph A. Allen from the Seventh Ward resigned the commissionership to take charge of the Reform school near Boston, Mass. Resolutions were entered on the records commending his work in the Board and in the schools since his connection with them, his interest in education at large, and his sympathy with children, with congratulations to the trustees and teachers of the Reform school, and especially to those who would be under his control and direction. Commissioner Allen had been one of the most zealous members of the Board since its beginning, and to him is largely due the credit of introducing the phonetic system into our schools.

The Board organized March 26, 1861, and re-elected the president and the clerk and superintendent. The budget was allowed by the Common Council, with $1000 added for a building fund, which relieved the Board from embarassment. Early in the season an addition was put on the west end of Townsend school-house two stories high, designed to seat 100 pupils. New and improved seats were put into Irving and Montgomery school-houses, a room was added to the Central Library in the City Hall, and provision made for the payment of all teachers.

In the autumn all arrangements were made for the transferring of the High school from the Pike block to the Greeley block, corner of Fayette and Warren streets, at a rent of $350.

The lecture course under the direction of the Board had been more extended in its influence than in preceding years, and at the March meeting resolutions of thanks were offered to the following speakers who had appeared : T. G. Alvord, N. B. Smith, Rev. M. E. Strieby, W. H. Shankland, Homer D. L. Sweet, Rev. S. J. May, Rev. Joseph M. Clark, Gen. Wm. J. Hough, Rev. James O'Hara, George L. Maynard, Finley M. King, and Dr. D. A. Moore. The annual report was printed in pamplet form.

On March 25, 1862, the new Board elected Lyman W. Conkey president, and on the 6th ballot re-elected Mr. Farnham clerk and superintendent. Several petitions for and against his re-election had been sent in.

Fees for tuition of non-resident pupils were increased, by which primary pupils were to be charged $7 a term, junior $8.50, senior $11.50, and High school $20.

A contract for the completion of the building on the lot bought last year, and also for raising Seymour school-house one story, was entered into for the sum of $6,800.

Mrs. Salisbury gave notice of her intention to retire from teaching at the end of the term in June. She had been a faithful, earnest, conscientious teacher for a long series of years, and had devoted herself to the best interests of her pupils. Her labors have been rewarded by the esteem and love of a large number of citizens who have grown to manhood and womanhood to do her reverence.

A contest that had arisen in the Board as to the propriety of preferring our High school graduates as teachers culminated in a resolution, "That where practicable High school graduates should have the preference." Since this time the spirit of this action has largely though not exclusively prevailed in the choice of teachers.

From the first the schools have lacked for room to seat all who apply for admittance, and this year, on account of the crowded condition of the primary rooms the plan was adopted of dividing first-year pupils into two classes, one-half to attend in the morning and the other in the afternoon. It has continued to the present time, probably not so much from an inability to provide sufficient sitting room, although that would have been difficult, as for the reason that for pupils five or six years old, half-day attendance is all that should be expected.

At the close of the year the report of the superintendent was adopted, and on account of the antagonism against him, resolutions were unanimously adopted by the retiring Board, strongly endorsing his work as superintendent and regretting the circumstances that required his retirement.

At the organization in March, 1863, Samuel L. Comstock was chosen president. For the position of clerk and superintenent there were three candidates, and the contest continued nearly two days ; at the 202d ballot Chas. E. Stevens received 5 votes and Mr. Farnham 3, and Mr. Stevens was declared elected.

An effort to make the salary of the clerk and superintendent $1,000, failed. Another division of the Board was manifested when the chairman of the teachers' committee reported the list of teachers with their salaries for the current year, Commissioner Leach of the Sixth Ward reporting another list for Townsend and Seymour schools. After a long contest the report of the teachers' committee was adopted as far as related to Genesee, Prescott, Clinton, Fayette, Putnam, Lodi, Irving and High schools, and an adjourment made to the next day, when the appointments were taken up by wards in numerical order. A petition signed by several residents of Jefferson school, asking for the appointment of Mr. Omer Leynes was received, but denied on the ground that such a course would lead to future embarrassment and increased expenditures. Jefferson school had been reduced to a junior grade at the opening of the new Salina school.

All appointments were finally made by the teachers' committee except the position formerly occupied by Mr. G. N. Harris of Seymour school. Commissioner Wellington made a motion to appoint Mr. Francis P. Hale, but another adjourment was effected and the matter left unsettled. At the next meeting two petitions were presented : one headed by L. H. Hiscock and 282 others, asking for the appointment of Mr. Harris ; and the other headed by Fairfax Wellington and 164 others asking for his removal. The final vote resulted in the choice of Mr. Hale as principal of Seymour school. Principal Harris like Superintendent Farnham had become unpopular, and the Board had undoubtedly been organized with reference to the removal of both. One cause of this determined opposition to Messrs. Harris and Farnham, was their active work in political caucuses and elections. They were well qualified for their respective positions, and had served the city faithfully and well. They should be honored for integrity and uprightness of character and for their zeal in doing what they considered their duty and privilege as citizens and educators. Mr. Farnham engaged in other fields of labor for about four years, and then accepted the position of superintendent of the Binghamton city schools where he remained several years. He afterward took the same position at Council Bluffs, Ia., and has but just resigned the principalship of the State normal school at Peru, Neb. He is well-known everywhere, not only as a teacher, but as the author of "The Sentence Method of Teaching Reading."

Mr. Harris opened a private school where for a few years he received better remuneration for his labor than the public school had given him ; but becoming tired of teaching he engaged in business and accumulated quite a property. Failing health compelled him to retire from all labor for several years and he died in 188-, honored and respected by all who knew him.

The new Genesee school-house lower floor was occupied in May for the first time. A room seating 50 pupils was rented for relieving Irving school, the library of Seymour school was seated, and an addition to the Putnam school-house was made at a cost of $1,000. These facts show the crowded condition of the schools at this period.

Miss Maria Welch, who afterward married Dr. Harris of Geddes, was appointed assistant in the High school and remained several years. Miss Marian Bushnell was appointed in Putnam school and has continued to this date in that and the central senior, Madison school and now is the principal of the Bassett school. She has been a faithful, earnest, conscientious teacher.

MISS MARIAN BUSHNELL.

The salary of the superintendent was

PASSETT SCHOOL.

raised during the summer to $1,200. Ansel E. Kinne resigned the principalship of Prescott school after a service of nine years, having been appointed superintendent of the Freedmen's Bureau of Florida.

The resignation of Mr. Kinne was accepted with regret, and appropriate and commendatory resolutions were passed relative to his success and faithfulness as a principal and a teacher. W. W. Raymond succeeded him.

Townsend and several other schools were found incapable of seating pupils who applied for admission, and the Common Council was solicited to take steps looking to an increase of the building fund.

In March a communication from Mr. Byrne asking, in conformity to the laws of 1850, that the St. Vincent de Paul Orphan Asylum children be allowed to participate in the public money. A committee of the Board with Mr. Byrne was appointed to prepare a case and present it to the Court for its decision in the premises, at the same time expressing a desire to comply with the request if legal to do so. This action did not result at that time in a favorable decision but at a later time, as will be seen, a satisfactory arrangement was entered into.

On March 24, 1864, the new Board re-elected the old officers. Steps were immediately taken for the enlargement of Jefferson, Townsend and Prescott schools.

Misses Clara A. Dean, Carrie G. Morris, and Mercia

Slocum, principals respectively of Montgomery, Irving and Clinton schools resigned, a n d their places were filled in order b y t h e appointment of Mrs. Marietta S. Avery, Mrs. Lucy M. Brand, Mrs. Charlotte B. Hurd.

MRS. LUCY M. BRAND.

The salary of the High school principal was increased $50, those of the ward male principals $100, those of women principals $50, and those of other teachers proportionately. The entire teaching force consisted of 5 men and 90 women.

Material was provided for illustrating length, weight and color in the primary department, the omission of physiology and the substitution of elementary geometry in the junior department.

A. G. Salisbury having received an appointment under the government, Theodore Camp was appointed his successor. ¡On accepting¿ Mr. Salisbury's resignation strong resolutions were adopted, setting forth the ability, the character, and the success of Mr. Salisbury as a teacher and citizen.

In July of this year the superintendent notified the Board that with present salaries, many of the teachers could not pay their living expenses.

A committee was appointed, and reported that the school funds must be put upon a broader basis than the present, in order to compete with schools in other cities, and to enable Syracuse to hire and retain such teachers as the educational interests of our city demands.

A special meeting was called in January, 1865, at which the Board took the following action :

"WHEREAS, The condition of our finances is such that it is, at present, beyond our power to grant this request : but, recognizing the necessity of such advance, therefore,

" *Resolved*, That upon the organization of the next Board of Education, we will use our utmost efforts and influence to have such advancement made and in such manner that the teachers may receive the benefits of the same for the present year."

Action was also taken toward amending the city charter, thereby giving the Council power to raise a greater sum to be applied to school purposes.

On March 28, 1865, the new Board elected Samuel J. May president. The increased duties of the clerk

JOHN H. FRENCH.

required so much time that the office of superintendent and clerk was divided. John H. French was chosen superintendent and principal of all the schools; and Charles E. Stevens clerk, each at a salary of $1,000.

At the opening of the spring term in May an advance in the salaries of all the teachers placed the compensation of the principal of the High school at $1,200; other men principals $1,000; women principals $450; and with those of assistant teachers increased in the same ratio. There were 107 teachers on the pay-roll. The entire seating capacity of all the schools was 4,450 and the number in attendance 4,400.

In September the superintendent, John H. French, resigned after five months' service to become the vice-principal and professor of theory and practice of teaching in the State Normal school at Albany for a short period, when he became State superintendent of schools of Vermont. He afterward became principal of the State Normal school at Indiana, Pa., and published a series of arithmetics which have had a wide circulation. For many years he had been widely known as an institute conductor, and he finally accepted a permanent position in the institute corps of New York, which place he filled at the time of his death in 1888. His funeral was held in St. Paul's church, and he was buried in Oakwood.

During the year Townsend and Seymour schools had by enlargements added to the seating capacity about 300.

CHARLES E. STEVENS.

At the organization in March, 1866, Rev. Samuel J. May was re-elected president; and on balloting for clerk and superintendent, Charles E. Stevens received four votes and Edward Smith, four votes. After the third ballot with the same result, Mr. Stevens withdrew his name and Mr. Smith was elected unanimously. This was within about four weeks of the end of the term and Mr. Smith continued as principal to its close, acting as superintendent before and after school and on Saturday, while Mr. Stevens was continued under pay attending to the work of clerk till the close of the term.

The Board of Education had drifted into the practice of providing funds to pay its expenses by making loans on its own account, and now such a loan was made for $18,000.

Another advance of salaries was made at the beginning of this school year, senior principals being raised to $1,200; junior to $500; with the same relative advancement for assistant teachers. The whole number appointed was 116. The course of study was revised and in the primary grades a system of object teaching was introduced. At the first examination of teachers under Mr. Smith's supervision, 38 entered and 21 passed the required 75% and received the certificates of the Board.

Among that number Miss Abbie Croly alone remains a teacher in the city schools at this date. Miss Eliza J. Leyden is now teaching in the high school at Newark,

N. J. Miss Maggie Dunn, now Mrs. Farnham, another of the class taught some years in Salina school. She is now a widow and resides in the First Ward. Miss Fannie Chesebro, now Mrs. Clark, taught in several schools with success, married and is now a kindergarten teacher in Keble school in this city. Ebenezer Butler, for a time principal of Seymour school, resigning to take charge of the schools at Whitehall, afterward returned to the city, and became principal in the village of Danforth, as already noted (p. 34). He is now in business in the city. There are others of that class living here or in the vicinity, but many of them are dead.

J. M. Bayne who had been teaching at Fayetteville with marked success was appointed principal of Salina school; but failing health obliged him to decline the position and E. M. Wheeler from New Boston was selected for the position.

In accordance with public sentiment expressed at a public meeting of citizens called for that purpose a formal application was made to the State Department for the establishment of a branch normal school in this city. The request was not honored, the idea at Albany being that a small country town was preferable.

The second monthly report of the superintendent announced the successful change from the phonetic to the phonic method of teaching in the primary department, good progress in the introduction of object teaching, the apparent good results from a change in the course of study, etc. Irving school had been enlarged during the year by an addition in the rear at a cost of $5,540 by which 100 more pupils could be seated. Provision was made for the payment of the principal of the Orphan Asylum school; only the assistant's salary had been paid hitherto.

On March 5, 1867, all the officers of the Board were re-elected. Early in the season a wood house on Lodi street, Second Ward, was purchased at a cost of $1,500 for a primary school. It was made ready for the beginning of the May term, and was the beginning of the Franklin school.

At a meeting on March 28, the use of corporal punishment in the city schools was prohibited. This action caused consternation among some of the teachers, and many of them had doubts as to the advisability of making public such a radical movement. Some of the teachers did not hesitate to say that all means for maintaining order had been taken from them. Instead of the calamities anticipated, the general discipline of the schools was improved and the atmosphere of almost every room became brighter. This regulation is now in force.

A contract for enlarging Montgomery school-house at a cost of $5,204 was made in June by which six additional rooms were secured. A lot was purchased on West Genesee street at a cost of $16,000 for a High school and plans were adopted for a building capable of seating 600 pupils ; providing rooms for the Central Library and rooms for the Board of Education. The contract was let to J. Grodevant for the sum of $51,950 and the building on the lot which he afterward sold for $1,500. The site of this school-house occupies in part the ground of the old red mill of early times. It was low and required much filling and a high stone wall to be built on the bank of Onondaga creek. The cost of this work was about $3,000.

A lot was purchased in the Second Ward, on Butternut street, for $4,250 ; and a lot in the Fifth Ward, between Otisco and Tully streets, containing 12 x 18 rods, was purchased for $4,700. The last two purchases were to be paid for in installments in from five to nine years.

Two ungraded winter schools were opened in the autumn of this year, Daniel Losey having in charge the one in the First Ward, and A. E. Kinne of one in the central part of the city. Both of these gentlemen having been in charge of senior schools in the city and known to possess superior ability were allowed the same salary as other male principals.

Principal T. D. Camp, of Putnam school, was compelled on account of ill-health to retire from the school that he might live in New York where he always enjoyed good health. Mr. Camp had been in Onondaga academy before his appointment to the Putnam school. He was

High School.

popular among his pupils and teachers, and but for fail-
ing health would have remained in this city. He was succeeded by Mr. Kinne. The Put-nam school has usually been fortunate in its teachers, and many of those formerly em-ployed are still resi-dents of Syracuse or vicinity. Among these may be named Mrs. W. W. Newman, formerly Miss E. E. Williams.

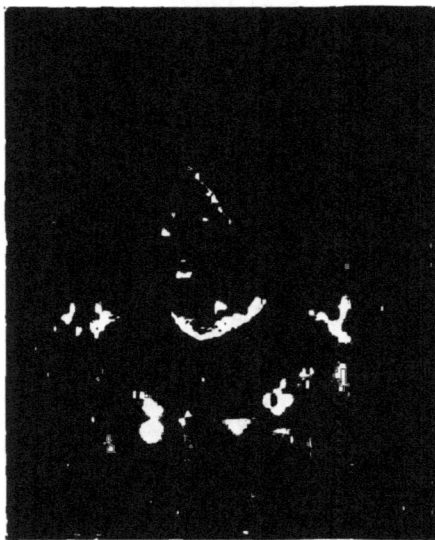

MRS. W. W. NEWMAN.

At the close of this year T. J. Leach, who had served in the Board four years retired with expressions of regret from all his associates.

CHAPTER IV

THIRD DECADE—1868 to 1877

In March, 1868, the Board organized by electing the old officers.

Another strong petition came to the Board from the Townsend district, asking that the school be made a senior school and a German teacher of high grade be employed. This called out a full report from a majority of the committee, consisting of S. J. May and Orrin Welch, against granting the request, mainly on the grounds that the language of our country is English and the common school should be confined to it; since the aim of our schools is to prepare for citizenship. John L. Roehner, the other member of the committee, gave a minority report favoring the request because his constituents desired an additional teacher of the German language. The majority report was adopted.

The superintendent reported twenty-three successful candidates from the annual teachers' examination and certificates were granted to them. Among the number was Mary L. Dwyre, who proved to be a superior teacher. She began work in 1868 in Montgomery school, and from there went to Putnam school, and after 17 or 18 years of successful teaching she asked leave of absence to attend the Cook County, Ill., Normal school, Col. F. W. Parker, principal. After completing her course there she returned to this city according to the conditions of the leave of absence, though she could have received a higher salary in the west. She is now in charge of the training school located in the Putnam building, where her influence and her systematic teaching are seen in the well-trained, competent teachers prepared for the future employment in our schools.

During the year May school building was erected by J. Grodevant at a cost of $15,875, unfurnished. When completed and ready for use the entire cost was over $20,000. A contract for seating the High school was made at the same time.

Invitations to the Board to attend the inauguration ceremonies of Cornell university were accepted and several members of the Board and superintendent were present. The high standing of this institution is largely due to the wisdom and scholarship of our townsman, Hon. Andrew D. White, its first president.

Late in the season a box came from Europe filled with books, and the following communication was sent to the Board :

" *To the Board of Education,*

' GENTLEMEN :—During our recent visit in Europe, recognizing our obligation to the educational interests

MAY SCHOOL.

under your control, and desiring to add to the usefulness and attractiveness of the excellent public library which you are now gathering, we obtained certain works which we have the honor to place in your hands, as a gift to our fellow-citizens. The first presents a full set of *The London Builder,* an illustrated periodical on architecture and engineering in twenty-four volumes folio. The second named presents a full set of *The London Illustrated News,* a periodical on contemporary art and history in fifty-one volumes folio. In the hope that these works, presenting as they do, not only news of the daily life of other nations, but also their most recent works on civil, domestic, church and school architecture, may be practically beneficial and a source of not only pleasure, but of profit, we remain, very respectfully and truly yours,

ANDREW D. WHITE,
BARRETT R. WHITE."

This gift was accepted and the president acknowledged it with the thanks of the Board.

The late Hon. Dennis McCarthy, our member of congress, also contributed eighty-one volumes of *The Congressional Globe* and appendix to the Central Library. A vote of thanks in behalf of the Board and citizens was unanimously passed.

In February, 1869, E. T. Zalinski, a former pupil of the High school, and then a lieutenant of the United States navy, sent a communication notifying the princi-

Robert Bruce White.

pal of the school that he had shipped to the superintendent a hogshead of coral, gathered personally by him at Key West, where he was stationed, in acknowledgment of the lasting benefit he had received while a member of that institution. This was received with thanks to the donor and the valuable specimens sent are now located in the cabinet in the High school building.

On account of abundance of room in the High school building and a lack of room in most of the ward schools, the two highest classes in the senior department were combined and transferred to the High school building, thus forming another school called the Central senior school and to occupy the second floor, while the High school would be located on the third floor. All senior schools except Salina were included in this arrangement, and A. E. Kinne was appointed principal, and R. B. White was appointed to Mr. Kinne's place in Putnam school.

Petitions for and remonstrances against the appointment of Mr. Roundy as principal of the High school were sent to the Board. This created quite an excitement for a few days, but resulted in the appointment of Mr. Roundy with a salary of $2,000. He was also given leave of absence for two weeks for the purpose of visiting similar high institutions. In November of this year a resolution was passed by the Board requiring a reduction in the salaries of teachers for absence from their schools for any other cause than personal sick-

N. B. SMITH.

ness. The reason for this was the supposed negligence
of some in the discharge of their duties.

Nearly at the close of this year St. Vincent de Paul
Orphan Asylum was placed under the supervision of
the Board on the same conditions as the Onondaga
County Orphan Asylum. A letter was received from
Rev. Mr. May, dated at Washington, D. C., resigning
his position as president of the Board on account of
increasing infirmaties and frequent absences from the
city.

Commissioner N. B. Smith, who had been acting as
president *pro tem.*, presented a paper recounting the
services rendered by Rev. S. J. May during his six years
of labor in the Board.   In all Mr. May's relations with
the Board, with the teachers, the scholars and parents,
he had proved himself just, kind and true ; and so
honest and serious were his purposes, that he rarely
failed in reaching right conclusions.   He was unwearied
in his labors, he looked after the capacity and welfare
of the teachers, gave attention to the erection and
repair of school-houses, kept himself informed of the
condition and wants of the library, and always aimed
to make the course of study complete and practical, so
as to be a fit preparation for a business life.   In one
respect Mr. May had failed in the accomplishment of
a long-cherished desire.   He believed that a reform
school for truant and refractory children was greatly
needed in our city and would have rejoiced to give his
time and attention to its establishment.

O. C. HINMAN.

Principal White resigned his position in Putnam school to engage in other business and O. C. Hinman was appointed to succeed him. Mr. White had been in the city schools one year and had secured the approbation and the respect of all who saw his power as a disciplinarian and a teacher.

In the autumn of this year Prof. Hart, a graduate of Cornell university, proposed to the Board on condition of having paid to him the sum of $200, to furnish a case of labelled minerals from Brazil for the cabinet, and a course of ten lectures before the city teachers and the Board. The sum was paid to Mr. Hart and he faithfully discharged his obligation the next season to his credit and the profit of his auditors. He also donated two cases of South American butterflies.

In the autumn plans and specifications for Franklin school were adopted and the contract let for enclosing the structure and finishing the lower floor at a contract price of $13,400. In the spring of 1871 Genesee school-house was raised one story at a cost of $5,150. This was largely done to provide a permanent place for ungraded and evening schools, where they were continued for a number of years and until the regular school required the room.

The 25th annual session of the New York State Teachers' Association was held in this city, July 26. The members of the Board, the superintendent, and a few other citizens were on the committee of arrange-

WALTER A. BROWNELL.

ments; and liberal gifts of money were raised among business men toward defraying the expenses. The session was largely attended.

Through a course of lectures held in the assembly-rooms of the High school $400 was raised for the purchase of a piano.

On January 27, 1871, Patrick McCarthy, the librarian, died after a service of many years. He was a conscientious, earnest and faithful employee, and did good work in organizing the Central Library. The Board passed fitting resolutions, and attended his funeral in a body.

Mr. Roundy having been for some time failing in health resigned his position in the High school, and a resolution highly approving of his work and expressing sympathy for his enfeebled health was unanimously adopted.

A. G. Salisbury was unanimously appointed temporary principal, and remained in the school to the close of the school year, when W. A. Brownell was made principal, at a salary of $2,500. After one year he was made teacher of natural science, being in turn succeeded at the same salary by Samuel Thurber of Massachusetts.

Up to this time the school year had been divided into three terms. It was now divided into two terms, examinations to be held at the end of each. An addition was made to Salina school at a cost of $2,500; and the lot was purchased for Madison school at $6,000. The old Franklin school on Lodi street was sold.

Principal J. B. Brigham resigned from Prescott school, and W. A. Welch was made his successor. In

WHEATON A. WELCH.

August a resolution was passed by the Board discontinuing the teaching of the German language in any city school except the High school. Miss Margaret Barber was made principal of Montgomery school. The Board adopted a regulation forbidding the use of any system of rewards either for deportment or lessons. The plans for the Madison school having been completed the contract was let to J. Grodevant for the sum of $17,500.

In October the Putnam school-house was destroyed by fire, the walls only remaining. In order to continue the school the C senior and A junior classes were transferred to the upper story of the Genesee building, the other junior classes to the Prescott school. Rooms for the primary department were secured on Salina street, on the second floor of the Washington block. A contract was entered into for the immediate repair of the Putnam building to be completed January 1, 1872.

The usual evening schools were opened in the fall; the First Ward school with Mr. Lawrence principal, and the central school with Daniel Losey as principal, assisted by J. B. Brigham and Rev. Mr. Miller. E. M. Wheeler who had served since 1866 resigned the principalship of Salina school and was followed by J. B. Brigham, five months after his resignation from Prescott school. Mr. Wheeler engaged in teaching in other places and in preaching. He was killed in the spring of 1892 by being thrown from a carriage.

H. P. Stark was, at his own suggestion, allowed to teach music in the primary department of Putnam school as an experiment and without compensation. This was the first systematic introduction of music into the public schools of this city.

Measures for enforcing vaccination were adopted and all pupils were required to be vaccinated.

Principal Welch resigned from Prescott school, after a service of one year, to take charge of Public School

MADISON SCHOOL.

No. 7, Brooklyn.   He was afterward transferred to No. 35, one of the largest in the city, and held this position at his death, November 3, 1892.   Miss Jennie Marlette also resigned.   She had been teaching about ten years : two in Jefferson school, five in Prescott school, one as principal of Montgomery, and two in the Central Senior school.   After leaving here she taught in Burlington, Vt., and married.

At the beginning of the year Chancellor Peck of Syracuse university came before the Board with a plan for establishing a preparatory university course of study in the High school "for the benefit of such pupils as may hereafter desire to attend that institution."   The proposition was not favorably received, on the ground that the High school is a part of the public school system and would be embarassed by having any part of the course of study directed or in any way controlled by a denominational institution.

The abandoned school premises known as the Fayette and the Lodi schools (Nos. 6 and 10) were sold and the proceeds applied toward the erection of the new Madison school.

After an existence of four years the Central Senior school was abandoned and the senior classes were sent back to their respective districts.

Some changes in the course of study were made this year among which was the limiting of technical grammar to a two years' course, confined to the last two years in the grammar schools, the year preceding to be devoted to oral teaching of language and sentential constructions.

The dividing of the school year into two terms had caused some friction at first. The High school had increased in numbers, and Principal Thurber recommended the adoption of semi-annual promotion as in the lower grades. Since then two classes have been received into the High school each year. Up to this time pupils had not been required to pass in every study of the Regents' preliminary examinations, but were frequently admitted conditionally. Now, however, 75% in all studies was required for admission, but if the pupil stood 75% on the average and fell below only in one study, and not lower than 65% in that he might be allowed to go on upon condition that his failure shall be made up during the first year.

In accordance with a circular of Gen. Eaton, Commissioner of the Bureau of Education, asking that all schools be represented at the Worlds' Fair in Vienna in 1873, preparations were made and completed early in the coming year for the presentation of such statistics as that circular required.

George F. Griffin, teacher of classical literature in the High school, and Principal J. B. Brigham of Salina school, resigned, and were followed by Giles F. Hawley and Daniel Ayers. Miss Mary F. Rhoades was appointed teacher of German in the High school.

ORRIN WELCH.

An effort, first proposed by Rev. Mr. May, but approved by nearly all members of the Board, had been repeatedly made to induce the city to inaugurate a reform school but the cost of starting and maintaining such an institution was considered too great a burden.

At the beginning of this year a suggestion was made that the Central ungraded school, which had been held only during the winter, be continued through the summer, and that irregular or refractory pupils from the ward schools be required to attend there. This was adopted by the Board and promised well for a time under the charge of Daniel Losey. But after a while, it became unpopular among parents who associated with it the stigma of a reform school. Late in the year it was abandoned. It lacked the authority of law for compulsory attendance.

In January, 1874, Daniel Ayres resigned the principalship of Salina school, and R. B. White, who had by his former record gained the confidence of the public, was made his successor.

Late in this season the High school suffered a loss by the death of Charles J. Foote, teacher of French. By his tact, industry, and enthusiasm he had kept up a good degree of interest in this branch of study, and by his practical methods and his earnestness, had stimulated other teachers to better work in their departments. His funeral was attended by the Board in a body, and appropriate resolutions were entered upon the records. Mrs. Foote was appointed his successor.

On March 4, 1874, Orrin Welch was elected president of the Board.

A petition was presented from several physicians asking for a change in the hours of the sessions of the High school on account of the health of pupils. After several trials of different hours it was finally settled that one session from 8:30 A. M. to 1:15 P. M. with a short recess was the best plan for the good of the whole, and essentially this arrangement has continued up to this time.

In June, a new election for librarian resulted in the choice of John S. Clark in place of Wm. McCarthy.

Lots were purchased and wooden buildings erected in the Fifth and Seventh Wards, at a cost respectively of $7,019.15 and $8,891.41. These are known as the Grace and the Adams schools. Jefferson school was also enlarged by an addition on the west side and by making it a three-story building, at a cost of $5,000. An outlay of $1,185.97 was put upon the Madison school lot for grading and fencing.

John F. Dee was appointed assistant clerk in place of Charles J. Miller. Giles F. Hawley resigned his place as teacher in the High school and Ebenezer Butler as principal of Seymour school. At the annual appointment of teachers, Joseph W. Taylor was appointed principal of Seymour school, Miss Myra Cool principal of Grace school, and Miss Mary Burke principal of Adams school.

OLD GRACE SCHOOL.

During this year the Walter Smith's System of Drawing was adopted, and the first general exhibition of this subject in the public schools was held in the High school building under the direction of Mrs. Mary D. Hicks, teacher of drawing in the public schools. Selections were made from every class in the city, and the work put upon suitable frames and tables where it could be easily examined.

E. F. Ballou, teacher of music, made a report, this being the close of the second year of the teaching of this branch in all the public schools of this city, in which he said that all grades above the primary could successfully analyze and perform the chromatic scale, and that by another year this subject would be thoroughly established and graded in the schools.

A feeling of insecurity as to the safety of some of the school buildings had become somewhat prevalent, and architects were employed to examine them. Some of these were strengthened, among them the Salina, Franklin, May, Seymour and Genesee buildings.

Another course of lectures was prepared and given by the High school pupils before large audiences in the autumn and the proceeds applied to the purchase of apparatus for the use of the High school. Prof. Brownell offered to the Board a large collection of minerals, classified and labelled for the cabinet for $150. This collection would bring a much larger sum, but something of the kind was needed for study of this subject. The offer was accepted.

ADAMS SCHOOL.

The new organization was affected March, 1875. W. A. Duncan was then elected president.

Ever since the organization of the High school there had been an element in our city in opposition to it as a free school maintained by tax. This year although the cost of maintaining that institution had been proportionally reduced from preceding years the same complaints were repeated. Principal Thurber, by request, prepared some statistics comparing the condition of the school in 1872 when he became principal with the present. There had been an increase of one teacher, and an increase of ninety-eight pupils. The salaries had increased 5% while the pupils had increased 60%. The course of study had been lengthened one year, thereby increasing the number of classes 25% ; while the cost of instruction was nearly 15% less in 1875 than in 1872. The income of the Board of Education for the benefit of the High school, beside the city appropriation, comes from two sources : 1st. Tuition from non-resident pupils; 2d. The Regents' appropriation, which is dependent upon the number of pupils holding Regents' certificates and styled academic pupils. In 1872 there were 134 such scholars, and in 1875 there would probably be 240, showing an increase of 106 or more than 79%. These facts plainly show that economy in conducting the expenses of the High school had been studied and that in comparison with other schools of the kind, in this or other States, it would be hard to find any more economically conducted.

W. A. Duncan.

On April 4th the Salina school house was burned to the ground, and the plans for a new building were adopted and the contract let for $14,256. The Common Council was asked to increase the sum for building purposes to meet this unexpected contingency. The pupils of Salina school were provided for temporarily by putting the primary department in the abandoned Catholic church of the First Ward, the junior pupils in Jefferson school, and the senior pupils in Genesee school.

The action of the Board by which an increase of $50 a year was added to the salary of the graduates of the High school who had spent one year in preparation for teaching was a stimulant for better prepared teachers.

An invitation to the Board to visit the bust of Rev. S. J. May by Miss Belle Gifford at the residence of J. L. Bagg, Esq., was received and accepted. Subsequently the following communication was received :

" *To the Board of Education of the City of Syracuse,*

"GENTLEMEN :—At a meeting last evening of the subscribers to the fund for the purchase of the marble bust of the late Rev. Samuel J. May, by Miss Belle Gifford, an artist of our city, and educated in our public schools, it was voted that the bust should be offered to the Board of Education of the City of Syracuse, to be placed in the Central library rooms of the High school building. With two exceptions, the subscribers to the fund are members of the religious society to which Mr. May was for more than twenty years the minister, and there was a very earnest wish on the part of many of them to place this beautiful work of art in their church edifice. But the deep interest which Mr. May took in the education of the people, his faithful and efficient services to the schools of the city, his long membership of your Board and the special aid which he rendered in the establishment of the High school and the erection of the beautiful building it occupies and where, if placed, the bust would be so much more accessible to the public, were controlling considerations in the decision which was finally made as to its disposition. At the same meeting a committee was appointed, of which the undersigned are members to communicate the action which was had to the Board of Education and to arrange with them for the transfer and reception of the bust.

Very respectfully,

W. BROWN SMITH,
N. C. POWERS,
Mrs. O. T. BURT,
Mrs. R. W. PEASE,
E. B. JUDSON,
DUDLEY P. PHELPS,
J. L. BAGG."

On September 18, 1875, the bust was placed in the middle alcove of the Central library, in front of the main entrance. The Rev. S. R. Calthrop, pastor of the Unitarian Society, in behalf of the donors, presented the bust to the city of Syracuse, to be in charge

of the Board of Education.   W. A. Duncan, president
of the Board of Education, in behalf of the citizens of
Syracuse and the Board accepted the bust, and introduced Hon. Andrew D. White, president of Cornell
university, as the principal speaker.   He gave a glow-
ing tribute to the character of Mr. May, and in closing,
said : " This bust would endure as a memorial of Mr.
May's character ; for the serene face would for years
radiate that benign influence which would cause some-
one to take up again the good work he had loved so
well."

In October of this year the Central ungraded school
was opened with Daniel Losey, principal, assisted by
A. B. Blodgett and George W. Hey ; and the evening
school under charge of J. Weed Monroe assisted by A.
S. Durston and A. B. Blodgett.   Later Mr. Blodgett
was transferred to the principalship of the First Ward
ungraded school, J. F. Belknap taking his place, and
James F. Steele becoming assistant in the First Ward
school.

The plan recommended by the Commissioner of Education at Washington for representing the city systems
of schools at the Centennial Exposition was adopted,
providing for a large card giving a synopsis of the public school system in respect to the subjects taught in
each grade, the number and designation of each grade,
with the number of pupils in each by sexes, the same in
respect to teachers, the salaries of teachers by sexes,

A. B. BLODGETT.

the population of the city, the taxable property, amount of taxes, school population, amount of school taxes, etc. Numerous items in relation to orphan asylums, private schools, business colleges, schools of pharmacy and dentistry, female colleges, Sunday schools, public libraries, art museums, scientific museums, associations for mutual improvement, including their character, number of members, value of libraries, collections, and instruments, etc.

The president in his inaugural recommended retrenchment as far as possible. Among other means for accomplishing this, all first year pupils might be limited to half-day attendance, half coming in the forenoon and the others in the afternoon. This had been in operation before, but was not strictly observed.

A reduction of about thirty assistant teachers from the preceding year had been made possible by consolidation and dividing the C primary classes ; but many of those dropped were employed before the expiration of the year, some on account of resignations and some because of large increase of pupils. A resolution was adopted reducing the salary of all High school teachers having $1,000 or upwards 10%.

In November the schools were closed for a week to give the teachers the opportunity of visiting the Centennial Exposition at Philadelphia. On account of the crowded condition of Prescott school one class of senior pupils was transferred to Genesee school, thereby making it partially a senior school. This has continued to the present time.

The ungraded schools in the First and Third Wards were opened in the fall under the principalships of Jas. A. Allis and James M. Gilbert respectively, and an evening school in Genesee school-house with J. Weed Monroe as principal.

The organization of the Board, March 6, 1877, was effected with no change in commissioners. J. W. Barker was elected president. The year beginning March 6, 1877, was marked by changes and reductions in salaries. Although last year the number of teachers had been reduced by more than thirty, and the salaries of High school teachers had been reduced 10%, the Common Council by a committee of conference with the Board of Education urged still greater reductions, but finally granted the sum asked for general purposes, disallowing the building fund.

E. F. Ballou, teacher of music, resigned, because of pressure upon the Board ; and George A. Bacon, assistant in the High school, was dropped by the Board from lack of funds. The High school course was reduced to a three-years' course.

The salary of assistant teachers were reduced, and that of the superintendent dropped to $1,800. Soon after the appointment of teachers, Principal Taylor resigned from Seymour school, and R. B. White was transferred to the position, A. B. Blodgett being appointed principal of Salina school. At a meeting in August the salary of male principals was made $1,200.

The basis of admission to the High school from the advanced A senior classes was made the same as for passing from the lower grades, *i.e.*, 75% in each study.

At the opening of the September term it was found necessary to employ more teachers in a number of the schools on account of the increased attendance.

Notwithstanding the strictest economy, as the year drew near its close, the funds were so limited that the clerk was instructed to write to the Superintendent of Public Instruction to ascertain the amount the city might expect from that source, and when it might be had. Notwithstanding the lack of funds the Board decided to open the evening school. J. Weed Monroe was put in charge, assisted by Michael E. Driscoll and Mr. Backman. Later in the season the ungraded schools were opened under the same supervision as in the preceding year.

The ladies of the Employment society asked for the privilege of using several of the school buildings for starting sewing schools in the different wards. The request was granted on condition that they be conducted without expense to the Board. A lady was appointed as overseer for each ward, under the supervision of the superintendent.

The High school had increased in attendance so that another teacher was needed, and George W. Rollins was appointed at a salary of $1,000.

CHAPTER V

FOURTH DECADE—1878 TO 1887

At a meeting of the Board, April 4, 1878, a memorial was adopted eulogizing Orrin Welch, lately deceased, for his long and useful service upon the Board.

Considerable attention having been attached to the schools of Quincy, near Boston, under the supervision of Col. F. W. Parker, a committee consisting of J. W. Durston and the superintendent was appointed to visit those schools to observe the work done by the pupils, the methods employed, etc.; and to report to this Board. The committee returned from the visit impressed with the personality and energy of Col. Parker, and with the results he had accomplished in the schools under his charge. He was filled with enthusiasm and energy and believed in breaking away from routine practices, in discarding everything which was merely formal in school methods, and in so con-

COL. F. W. PARKER.

EDWARD E. CHAPMAN.

ducting all school work as to stimulate observation and awaken thought. His most efficient work, at that time, had been directed toward better methods in teaching reading, spelling and arithmetic, and in doing this work to throw the burden of it upon the pupil. Composition and sight-reading were included in language, and common business transactions in arithmetic. The course of study was revised, and some of the principles advocated by the superintendent and teachers of the Quincy schools incorporated. Miss Belle Thomas, a Quincy teacher, was made principal of the primary department in Madison school.

Miss Mary P. Rhoades asked leave of absence that she might spend a year in travel abroad, and Mr. Thurber resigned the principalship of the High school, to accept a like position in Worcester, Mass. The Board passed resolutions highly commendatory of Mr. Thurber's character and work. George A. Bacon was appointed to succeed him.

In the autumn, Andrew D. White made another donation to the Central library, consisting of photographs of ancient Syracuse.

A lot on Willow street costing $2,500 was bought for Prescott school, in anticipation of a new building.

Commissioner Barker, who retired from the Board at the close of the year, had served as representative of the Third Ward for twelve years, and as the president of the Board for the last year. His services were

OLD MONTGOMERY SCHOOL.

acknowledged by appropriate resolutions. On March 4, 1879, the new Board elected Edward E. Chapman, president.

The Common Council having failed to make provision for carrying on the schools, the Board in May made a movement to continue the spring vacation indefinitely, but matters having been satisfactorily adjusted, the schools commenced at the usual time. Montgomery school had been improved during the summer vacation by changing recitation rooms into class rooms, and by adding to the building, additional entrances and stairways.

Penmanship had not been satisfactorily taught, and C. R. Wells after two months' trial was employed as special teacher. He continued in this position till the close of the year 1891–92, when he resigned to be enabled to accept the calls that came from cities in all parts of the country for special instruction. The "movement system" which he originated and developed in the schools of Syracuse is working a revolution in the teaching of this subject. Superintendents have wondered at the results obtained in our schools, and have visited us to see our methods, in every case returning convinced that the movement system is the one method of teaching. It is safe to say that in penmanship Syracuse leads every city in the country.

Owing to the deficiency of funds and also to the small and irregular attendance of the Central ungraded

Charles R. Wells.

school it was abandoned, but the First Ward school was opened under the charge of Mr. Allis.

Mrs. Mary Dana Hicks, who for a long time had been in charge of drawing in the High school and in the w a r d schools and who had been eminently successful in her work by raising the standard and popularizing this branch, resigned her place here, to accept a position in the Prang Publishing Company, of Boston. Her resignation was accepted with deep regret, and Miss Lucy A. Adams was elected to take her place in that department in the High school.

LUCY A. ADAMS.

In January, 1880, Miss Sophia C. Wightman resigned the principalship of May school after long service as a teacher in the employ of the Board. She was a faithful teacher, conscientious in her work and eminently successful, but failing health required rest, and death soon followed.

PRESCOTT SCHOOL.

The contract for the new Prescott school was let for $19,476 and the Seymour addition for $2,529.75. These amounts exceeded the appropriation and the Common Council was asked to increase the amount for building purposes.

Mrs. Gambia resigned her position as librarian and Rev. E. W. Mundy succeeded her at a salary of $1,000. The resignation of Miss Mary P. Rhoades from the High school was a loss much to be regretted. She had proved herself a teacher of uncommon power and influence, and her services would have been retained had the funds permitted. She went to the Brockport Normal school where her influence is strong and uplifting. Wm. B. Harlow, a graduate of Harvard, was appointed to succeed her.

Dr. Brownell was allowed $200 toward expenses in procuring specimens for the cabinet and for work in classifying and arranging specimens already there.

The Training school opened in September under a more systematic plan, in charge of Miss Belle Thomas, in the Madison school. Eight students entered the class and in January they were examined by a committee appointed by the Board. The examination tested the method of conducting a recitation ; power to hold the attention of children, in reading, writing, language ; and ability to lead pupils to discover the facts the teacher wished them to see, without suggestions from the teacher. This was the beginning of a teachers'

Rev. E. W. Mundy.

WM. B. HARLOW, PH. D.

class where specific training was given in all its details by one trained in the work.

Later in the season O. C. Hinman resigned the principalship of the Putnam school and John D. Wilson from Manlius succeeded him.

In the fore part of January, 1881, the Board attended the funeral services of Hon. Jas. Noxon who was a member of the first Board of Education and served in that capacity two years, (1848–49). Appropriate resolutions were entered upon the records.

On account of reports greatly detrimental to the character of the principal of Prescott school he resigned his position and W. P. Browning of Niagara Falls was appointed to succeed him. He declined the position and J. E. Hornis a teacher from Milwaukee accepted it. He soon after resigned, and A. B. Blodgett was transferred from Salina school. To the latter position H. E. Barrett, a graduate of the Oswego Normal, but at that time a resident of Chittenango and editor of a local paper, was appointed.

The new Prescott building was constructed with reference to being heated by steam, but strong opposition on the part of some members of the Board was made to this mode of heating on account of greater expense. The opposition prevailed and furnaces were substituted.

After eight years of service, the last two of which he served as president, Commissioner Edward E. Chap-

JOHN D. WILSON.

H. E. BARRETT.

man retired from the Board. He left with expressions of sincere and hearty thanks from all his co-laborers for his helpful, earnest work.

At the organization in March, 1881, H. R. Olmsted became president.

On account of a report that the Irving school had become unsafe, the front walls and sides were torn down, and practically a new building resulted. Putnam and Townsend schools were enlarged and partially remodeled this year, at a cost respectively of \$3,189 and \$817.33. In May of this year the senior department moved into the new Prescott school-house and the other departments the following month.

In October, George W. Rollins resigned his position as teacher of languages in the High school, to accept a position in Boston, and was followed by J. M. Griffin. Miss Ellen Williams, teacher of German, resigned, and Mrs. Emma Kingsley and Miss Carrie Shevelson were appointed. Dr. Bacon having received a call to a better position was induced to decline the offer by having his salary advanced to \$2,500. Mrs. A. E. Kinne resigned her position in Madison school on account of failing health.

William A. Sweet sent a communication to the Board, offering to pay the salary of a teacher for an evening school in the Fifth Ward on condition that suitable room and other conveniences were provided. Prin-

H. R. OLMSTED.

TOWNSEND SCHOOL.

cipal R. B. White was put in charge, and many young men profited by the experiment.

Commissioner J. H. Durston of the Eighth Ward resigned and D. L. Pickard was appointed in his stead. Mr. Pickard had previously served four years in the Board and was cordially welcomed back again. At the request of the State Board of Health, located at Albany, an elaborate and full report of the condition of the school-houses was sent to them, and upon the receipt of the same, Dr. Elisha Harris, State commissioner, returned thanks and asked permission to print portions in their annual report.

Our city suffered another loss by the resignation from the training school of Miss Belle Thomas, she being called to Geneva to take charge of a primary school. After Miss Thomas left, the superintendent took charge of the work as well as he could in justice to his other duties, which had now become greater than one man could satisfactorily perform. He reported to the Board in detail the work of that school, stating that he had continued it, but in order to make it successful a competent teacher must be employed and the course re-arranged with the work systematized and put upon a permanent basis.

After the organization of the new Board, Commissioner Duncan called up the request made by the principals the preceding June for a restoration of salary to the same that it had been five years before. This was

D. L. PICKARD.

adopted for all those who had been in the employ of the Board for three years. The commissioner also called attention to the condition of Seymour school-building, and asked for a careful consideration. He said almost the temporary repair fund for that ward for several years had been expended on that house in putting in piers, columns and bolts. Three times the building had settled several inches, and had been raised by screws to near its original position. It seemed to him useless to continue to expend money on the old structure. It was money thrown away. The executive committee by instruction from the Board proceeded to get plans and estimates for its improvement. At a meeting March 21, the committee reported that they had visited all the school-houses, and found several of them out of repair owing to short appropriations in past years. A much larger sum of money would be required to replace worn out floors, roofs, walks, outbuildings, paint, etc. It would be necessary to call for larger amounts for fuel, supplies, and for contingencies and teachers' wages. The committee also reported that Seymour school-house had been abandoned upon the demand of citizens of the ward, whose judgment was coincided with by all who had examined the building. Temporary provision for seating the pupils had been provided in such rooms in the ward as would accomodate them. Thus the school was continued but in most cases by very unsatisfactory surroundings.

The report having prevailed that pupils were suffering from too great a strain upon their eyes, Dr. Van Duyn with the superintendent was appointed to visit the schools and report to the Board. It was found in one of the best that not more than 3% of the pupils in any room had any defective eye-sight, and that this had not increased in the higher grades. This was not true of some of the other schools. Test-type was recommended for the trial of the eyes of the children by the teachers, so that pupils might be seated in accordance with their power of vision.

In May, bids for a new building for the Seymour

Mrs. LIBBIE I. BROWN.
Prin. Primary Department, Seymour School.

school were opened and found far to exceed the appropriation. A committee from the Board was appointed to consult with the lowest bidder for the purpose of devising some way for going on with the w o r k, if possible. The Common Council passed a resolution to give $25,000 to the b u i l d i n g

SEYMOUR SCHOOL.

fund if that would fully equip the house for school purposes.

Plans were revised, and a contract entered into with A. L. Mason to enclose the building for the sum of $15,700, including an addition on the north-east corner for recitation rooms.

Mrs. C. B. Hurd, who had long served as a faithful, competent and successful teacher, resigned from Clinton school on account of failing health and Mrs. L. L. Goodrich supplied her place.

On March 6, 1883, William Brown Smith was elected president of the Board. Mrs. Lucy M. Brand, after a long and faithful service as a teacher, covering a period of twenty-seven years, having been principal of Salina, Irving and Genesee schools, successively, sent to the Board her resignation. This was accepted with grateful acknowledgment of her excellent service.

Just before the adjournment Commissioner Duncan called the attention of the Board to the fact that this closed the seventeenth year of consecutive service by Mr. Smith as superintendent of schools of this city, that this was probably the longest time any one in the State had held such a position, and that no one not connected with school work could appreciate the difficulties incident to the position ; ten thousand children must be cared for during ten months of the year ; schoolhouses needed constant watching in matters of safety and health ; teachers were to be trained, guided and

WILLIAM BROWN SMITH.

helped, and matters of discipline settled. In all this vast matter of detail all recognized Superintendent Smith's position, integrity, watchfulness and faithfulness. He therefore moved a vote of thanks, which was seconded by Commissioners Smith, Olmstead and Pickard in brief remarks, and unanimously adopted.

At the appointment of teachers in June Miss S. M. Arnold received the appointment for one term, which would end in January, 1884, and the clerk was instructed to notify her to this effect. Miss Arnold was expected to give in her resignation, but this she failed to do, reporting herself at the beginning of the following term, and she had been in the school one month at the organization of the new Board. A special meeting was called to consider her case, when it was decided to let her continue to the end of the year. She was then made principal of the primary department of Montgomery school.

Action was taken allowing pupils preparing for entrance to the High school to take the Regents' examination in spelling and geography at the close of the first half of the eighth year, and the examination in grammar and arithmetic at the end of that year.

The salaries of the senior principles was advanced to $1,500.

Mrs. Mary J. Perry who had served three or four years as teacher in two of the ward schools and several years as an efficient and zealous teacher in the High school, after a severe illness was removed from her labors by death.   The Board adopted resolutions strongly commending her faithful work.

Upon reviewing the finances it was found that barely enough money remained at the disposal of the Board to pay the salaries of teachers now under contract, while there were now seven schools, each of which needed an additional teacher.   On motion, the president and clerk were instructed to prepare a statement to present to the Common Council setting forth these facts.   Later in the season the commissioner in each of the wards with the superintendent put in additional teachers where they were needed for one month.

Several meetings were held by the Board, and two joint meetings of the Board and Common Council in relation to providing additional funds for carrying on the schools to the close of the fiscal year ; and upon the failure of the Council to provide these, the schools were closed January 24, 1884, by the following resolution :

" *Resolved*, That the Superintendent be instructed to give notice to the principals of the schools and through them to the teachers, that the schools will be closed until further notice, except the Regents' classes now in examination, which will continue to its close ; and that the superintendent be instructed to notify the mayor of this action.

" *Resolved*, That the president of this Board be requested to notify the public, through the press, of the reason for this action."

The mayor responded by saying that necessary funds would be provided. This action resulted in calling the Board together immediately and the clerk was instructed to notify the mayor that when the Board shall be informed that sufficient funds have been placed in the city treasury for carrying on the schools they will be opened. Another reply was received in response notifying the Board that funds to the amount of $3,750 had been placed in the Merchants' National Bank to the credit of the Board of Education. This called another special meeting January 24, 1884, when the following reply was ordered:

"*To the Hon. Thomas Ryan, Mayor of the City of Syracuse,*

"DEAR SIR :—Your official communication, notifying the Board of Education that you had placed $3,750 to their credit in the Merchants' National Bank, is received. Assuming that this money will be transferred to the city treasury, from which alone we are authorized to draw, the schools will be ordered opened this morning. (Signed),

CLERK BOARD OF EDUCATION."

A full detailed statement of the financial condition accompanied the comunication to the mayor, showing a deficiency of $8,690, upon accounts already received which might be reduced by sums estimated to be received from the Board of Regents and from receipts from tuition of non-resident pupils, amounting altogether to $2,490, leaving still a deficiency balance of $6,200.

March 24 closed the fiscal year which had been one of more than common difficulties and trials, but all of which had been bridged over by leaving a debt for the next Board to provide for.

Janitors were required to have charge of the buildings for the entire year, including all vacations.

A committee from the Women's Temperance Union, at a regular meeting of the Board, presented a request from their organization asking for an introduction into the schools of a text-book on temperance. This was introduced, action having previously been taken on the matter.

At the organization of the Board, March 4, 1884, William Brown Smith was re-elected president but declined to serve and D. L. Pickard was elected. The arrearages from the preceding year caused much anxiety at the beginning of this year, and the budget was made up by placing at the head of it the amount of said arrearage and asking:

For last year's over-draft,	$ 6,989.58.
For teachers' wages,	97,500.00.
For other expenses,	39,400.00.

Of which sum the city was asked to raise 11,857.91, and for a permanent fund to cancel two mortgages on the Prescott school lot, one for $2,000 and the other for $1,800 making a total of $3,800. The Common Council approved the budget except the over-draft, which was claimed to be out of their power, and they recommended that the Board of Education unite with them in asking the Legislature to authorize the adding of the deficiency to the tax-list of this year. This course was finally adopted.

At the May meeting, the superintendent called the attention of the Board to the employment of children between the ages of eight and fourteen, in violation of State law. He further referred to the keeping of children after school for idleness, truancy, misconduct, etc. Both of these subjects received attention, the former by printing the statutes on cardboard and placing them in factories and other places where such children are employed and by calling attention of employers to the subject; and the latter by direct work among the teachers.

Mrs. L. L. Goodrich, principal of Clinton school, having prepared and mounted the ferns of Onondaga county, spread them on the tables of the Board for their inspection at the June meeting. She also sent a letter from which these extracts are taken :

" Gentlemen of the Board of Education,

"'Three years ago I sent to the H i g h school at Ottawa the

MRS. L. L. GOODRICH.

CLINTON SCHOOL.

mounted specimens of *Filius Onondaguesis*. Not feeling satisfied with myself in working for foreign missions when our own High school had no herbarium, I set myself to work to make a collection of all the ferns of this county for our own home institution, which I have collected from far and near, from rocks and mud, from hill and valley, and thoroughly studied, identified and mounted, and now, with pleasure, present them to you, hoping these will prove as those did I sent to Ottawa, a nucleus to a herbarium, not only of the flora of our own county, but of the State."

Mrs. Goodrich received the thanks of the Board, and the results have proven the wisdom of the giver in the work of the classes under the care and guidance of Miss Overacker, into whose charge the specimens were placed.

During the summer vacation the Madison schoolhouse was remodeled, heated and ventilated. This house, had from the first suffered in these respects. In the remodeling, large rooms were partitioned into smaller ones, making twelve rooms of sufficient size to seat from forty to eighty pupils each, all so arranged as to have good light, well heated and ventilated.

The Salina senior school was retransferred to the old building, and Miss Mary L. Ford was made principal of Jefferson school in place of Miss Freeman, who had resigned.

Timothy J. Cooney, who had acted as assistant in the superintendent's office, after a long and trying sickness, died, h a v i n g faithfully served in that capacity for more than seven years. T h e Board acknowledged their appreciation of his faithful services a n d his conscientious, upright character in resolutions

MARY L. FORD.

placed on the minutes of the meeting in August.

In the autumn of this year the village of Carthage was destroyed by fire, the school-houses together with the books and clothing of the children being destroyed. A letter from Superintendent George F. Sawyer to the city superintendent setting forth the necessities of the schools and the inability of the citizens to supply that need resulted in a collection from each of our city schools, amounting in all to $680.08.

Mrs. Goodenough being present at a teachers' meeting about that time gave some examples of vocal drill and offered to teach classes. Some of the teachers wishing to take lessons in this branch, she was temporarily employed at $40 per month, but after a short time the class was discontinued.

A committee appointed to look into the statutes relating to compulsory education, presented a full report, giving the text of the different acts of the Legislature relating to cities. The daily papers were requested to publish these for the enlightenment of the public. In January, 1885 a report by the superintendent was given of the condition of each of the school buildings, in respect to ventilation. Tests were made by means of the anemometer, and were considered reliable. Four or five of the houses were reported fair to good, and the remainder as requiring the attention of the Board for remodeling or rebuilding.

At the beginning of the term in February the senior departments in most of the schools were full, some of them not having room enough to seat all the pupils. Miss Estella Kneeland resigned from the High School and Miss Edith M. Clarke was appointed to the position.

Miss Kneeland was a graduate of Mount Holyoke Seminary, and a teacher of rare attractiveness and power. She married Fred C. Eddy, now cashier of the Bank of Syracuse. She is at this time president of the Portfolio Club, one of several literary organizations that have done much for the culture of the city.

Miss Mary Burke the former principal of the Adams school, and who had resigned on account of failing

MICHAEL MALONEY.

health some time before, died in January, 1885. On February 5, Miss Irene A. Clark succeeded her as principal. Miss Burke commenced teaching in 1858 in the Townsend school, after two or three years being transferred to the Putnam school as principal of the primary department. She continued in this school till the Adams school was built in 1874, when she was appointed its principal, which position she held till a few months before her death. She was very energetic and had the close co-operation of her teachers and pupils.

An effort was made by the commissioner of the Sixth Ward to secure a new school-house, and for that purpose a lot on South Salina street, near the crossing of the D. L. & W. Railroad, was contracted for, but the project was abandoned.

At the close of the fiscal year, Commissioner Warner offered the following :

WHEREAS, It appears from the statement of the clerk and from the report of Mr. Mann that the practice of having, in our financial year, the salaries of teachers, janitors and other officers of the Board begin February 1, instead of March 1, has existed since 1864, and as the reason for this seems to us more than over-balanced by the propriety of having all parts of our financial expenditures begin and close at the same time as in the other departments of the city government, therefore,

" *Resolved*, That we recommend to our successors to increase the amount of the budget, for the coming year to such a sum as shall be sufficient for school purposes from March 1, 1886, to March 1, 1887, with the addition of such an amount as shall be necessary to pay all officers' and teachers' salaries for the month of February next, to the end that all parts of our financial expenditures shall close hereafter March 1.

On March 1, 1886, Commissioner Maloney was elected president. Another standing committee, a committee on hygiene was added making eight in all.

The principals of the junior and primary schools had asked for an increase in their salaries during the last year which could not be allowed because no appropriation had been asked to meet such an expense, but at the beginning of this year their salaries were fixed at $800 and a sum needed to meet the advance was added to the budget which included :

The amount for salaries for last February, $ 10,309.30.

For teachers' wages from March 1, 1886 to
    March 1, 1887,   104,969.50.

And for increase in junior and primary
    principals' salaries,   7,095.86.

The total amount asked for teachers' sala-
    ries was   112,374.66.

All other expenses would require,   44,008.00.

The amount to be raised by the city,   129,958.45.

The Common Council reduced this last amount to $118,579.31. This action compelled the Board to re-adjust the budget by making pro rata reductions on each item included in the budget. Some dissatisfaction was felt on account of high salaries, and as one of these in the High school seemed to be out of proportion to the others, Mr. Brownell's was reduced to what it had been previous to the last advance, i. e. to $1,800. This was taken as a reflection upon Mr. Brownell and at the next meeting he and his friends secured its restoration to $2,000.

A special teacher was recommended for reading and vocal drill, and soon afterward Mrs. Goodenough received an appointment to drill the teachers for the remainder of that term.

The committee on hygiene after quite a thorough examination of all the schools made a full report of the hygienic conditions of each. The majority were found to be fair, but quite a number and especially the older buildings were condemned. The Montgomery house being built on low, flat ground was the worst of all. All the new buildings were satisfactory.

Miss Catharine Carrier of the Franklin school who had been in the public schools as teacher since 1869 almost without the loss of a day, was taken sick last term and asked for leave of absence. She was never able to resume her work and died in 1886. Appropriate resolutions as to her worth, faithfulness and success were entered upon the records.

As the year advanced and the schools filled up, the necessity for more school room became apparent. The

Clinton school was divided into small rooms to increase its capacity and newly seated. A new building in the Third Ward, named the Frazer school, was built at a cost when completed of nearly $20,000. On account of some unavoidable changes a greater expense was put upon this house than was expected and a supplementary budget amounting to $5,148 was asked of the Common Council.

On account of poorly ventilated houses, members of the hygiene committee visited Boston to see the method used there in some new houses by which with a fan driven by power almost perfect ventilation had been secured. This method was put into the High school in the fall at a cost of $2,197, and has proven a partial success, although not equal to what it might be in a house built for it. This plan has been used in three of the school-houses in this city, but it is regarded by the Board as too expensive and too liable to get out of repair unless great outlay is made at the beginning.

Mrs. M. L. McLean, principal of Townsend school, from an accident the preceding winter, caused by a fall, had been unable to be in her place and it was supplied temporarily. Later in the season she resigned and Mrs. Kate M. Cullen was appointed the principal. Mrs. McLean, first appointed in 1859 as M. L. Adams, was remembered at her death by suitable resolutions in regard to her character, her long service and her success.

Milton F. Griffin sent in his resignation as teacher in the High school, and is now teaching in the west. He was an excellent teacher beloved by all. Frederick Howard was appointed to succeed him.

MRS. KATE CULLEN.

During the summer vacation the Franklin schoolhouse had been remodeled and partially finished and supplied with new desks by which its seating capacity had been greatly increased. At the beginning of the term the Clinton, Grace, Seymour, Montgomery, Putnam, Irving and Madison schools in one or more departments were very much crowded. The demand for more room was so imperative that the clerk was instructed to write to the State Superintendent to ask him if it would be expedient for the city to exclude from the public schools children between five and six years of age. He replied, the State law allows children five years of age to attend the public schools, and the State pays public money to all districts for children of that age. They cannot therefore be legally excluded.

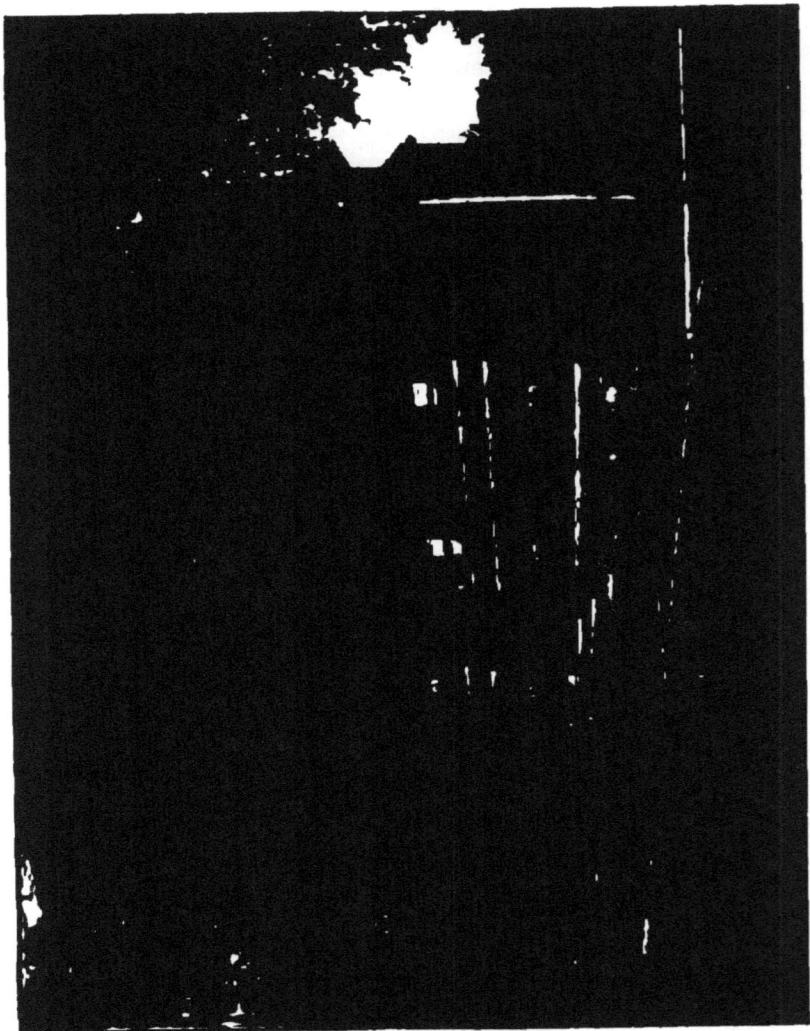

PUTNAM SCHOOL.

Preparations were made for a new building in the Putnam district and a lot was purchased on the corner of Madison and Mulberry streets at a cost of $15,000. A building of two stories containing sixteen rooms was commenced, and completed the next year. The contract price was $33,390, without seating, heating, walks, etc.

In 1886, the Board adopted a resolution requiring all female teachers upon marrying to send in their resignations. This was regarded by many as an unwise step, from the fact that nothing prepares a woman so well to train children in school, as the love and sympathy that is developed by the relation of mother and children in the family. The plea for the movement was that so many young ladies with no means of earning a livelihood had prepared themselves for teachers, and there were no places for them.

At this time the villages of Geddes and Danforth were annexed to Syracuse, adding to the city the Porter, the Gere, the Brighton, the Danforth, and the Rock schools.

The Board granted Dr. Bacon leave of absence without loss of salary through the months of May and June, that he might study up secondary education in Europe. Charles E. White, superintendent of the Geddes schools previous to the annexation of that village to the city, was appointed principal of Franklin school, and Miss Eliza Kennedy was trans-

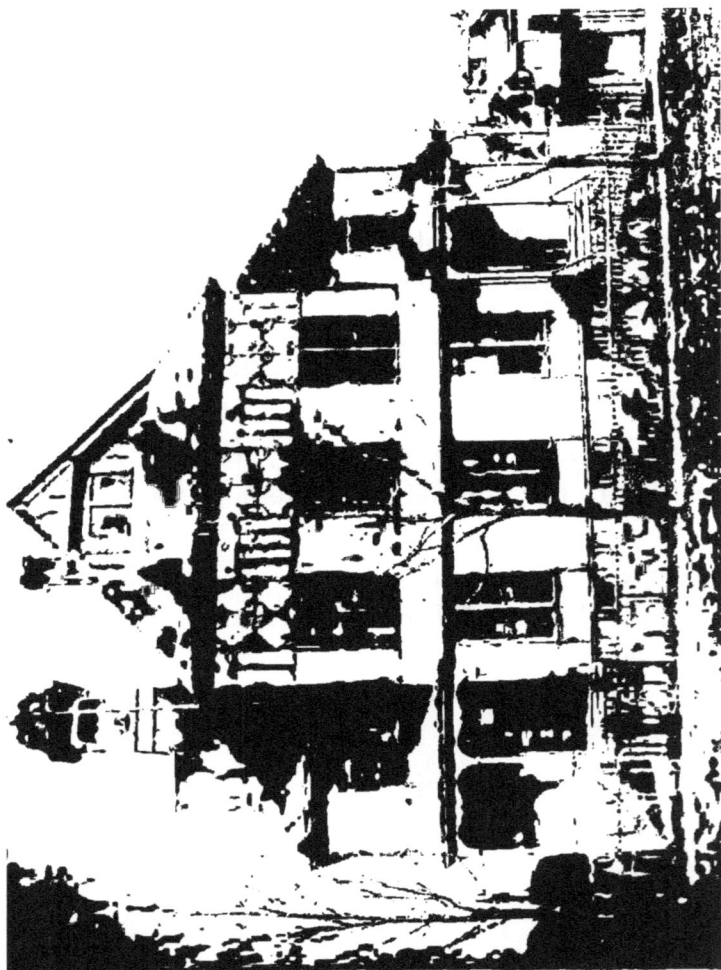

GERE SCHOOL.

VINE SCHOOL.

ferred from Franklin to the principalship of Frazer school. The name of the Central school in Geddes was changed to Porter school, in honor of Dr. Porter, who had formerly been a teacher there and afterward for many years one of the most useful and enthusiastic members on the Board of Education in the village.

Since the resigation of Mr. Ballou in 1876, there had been no regular teacher of music, but upon the adoption of the Normal course in music [1888], F. A. Lyman was appointed teacher and has been for four years in the work to the satisfaction of all connected with the schools.

Miss Eliza Caldwell, a teacher in the Danforth school, having been employed a few months, beginning in the autumn of 1886, was not doing satisfactory work, being somewhat erratic in her methods, and the commissioner of the Sixth Ward, under whom she was employed, although in a school where the commissioner of the Eleventh Ward had jurisdiction, notified her that her work was not satisfactory, and asked her to hand in her resignation. She appealed to the commissioner of the Eleventh Ward, and a special meeting of the Board was called to consider the matter. After hearing the matter it was decided to let her remain till the close of the term.

Another large tract joining the city on the south was annexed to the city. Most of this was a farming country but there was a small wooden house, of one room,

FRANKLIN SCHOOL.

CHARLES E. WHITE.

FREDERICK A. LYMAN.

on a lot to which the district had no title. A new lot was purchased, the building moved upon it and put in repair, and Miss Bessie Hurd appointed teacher, although there were only from fourteen to eighteen scholars.

In 1886, a lot was purchased in the Fourth Ward, and a four-room building of wood put upon it, designed to seat 200 pupils. Previous to this building a school had been kept in that locality in rooms rented for the purpose, which were inconvenient, small and unhealthful. The new building is on a good sized lot, on high ground, and with pleasant surroundings.

Principal Giles H. Stilwell and wife, of Porter school, resigned, Mr. Stilwell designing to enter the profession of law. Since then he has been admitted to the bar, and has made rapid strides in his profession. He is serving his fourth year as a member of the Board of Education, and is now the president of the Board. He was succeeded in Geddes by W. H. Scott. Principal Ebenezer Butler, of the Danforth school, resigned his position, and J. Q. Adams, from the Brighton school, became his successor.

The regular schools in the Fifth Ward were too full to admit all pupils desiring to attend, and a branch school was opened in the southern part of the ward, and styled the Merrick school. Rooms in the basement of a church, large enough for eighty pupils were fitted up. Being on low ground, high water in the

W. H. SCOTT.

J. Q. ADAMS.

spring compelled a removal to better quarters.   Since then a new, pretty, commodious house has been erected, with the Smead system of ventilation and closets, which has for two years given satisfaction.

The commissioner of the Tenth Ward urged that the higher department already established in the Porter school, be allowed to continue as it had been for three or four years, but this was not considered to be for the best interests of the children of that locality, and it would necessarily add materially to the expenses of the city.   The superintendent was directed to remove the apparatus belonging to high school work to the Syracuse High school.

Principal R. B. White wishing to engage in other work for a while and yet not to give up his position, asked for leave of absence.   This was granted, and Bruce M. Watson, a teacher of the High school, was given the place.   Mr. White did not return to this school, but two years after was appointed principal of the Madison school.   Mr. Watson has done excellent work, and Seymour school has maintained its standing under his administration.   Mr. Cummings followed Mr. Watson in the High school as teacher of the training class with success, but resigned at the end of a year to complete his college course of study in New Jersey.

In February a report of the teachers' committee in respect to the salary of lower grade teachers was accepted by which assistants for first year's service should receive

MERRICK SCHOOL.

BRUCE M. WATSON.

$300, for second year $350, for third year $400, and for fourth year and thereafter $450.

O. C. Kinyon was appointed teacher in the High school in place of Miss Shevelson, to whom had been granted leave of absence. Upon the return of Miss Shevelson the classes had so increased that Mr. Kinyon's appointment was made permanent.

Near the close of the fiscal year, books, sets of drawing models, pencils and stationary for the use of primary children were purchased at a cost of $2,331.33. This purchase had been made possible by a change in the city charter providing for the supply of all books and other material in the primary department.

A. VON LANDBERG.

CHAPTER VI

FIFTH DECADE—From 1888

In March, 1888, Alexander Von Landberg was elected president of the Board. The superintendent recommended a re-adjustment of the grades in the city schools by naming them primary, grammar, and High school, but no action was taken. The reasons given for making the change were that the Bureau of Education required such a division and this would not interfere with State reports. It would also be in harmony with the New England system of reporting and with that of several of the other States.

At the appointment of teachers in June for the next school year, Miss Lizzie Dwyre was made principal of the primary department of Montgomery school, and Miss Arnold assistant.

On July 5, 1888, Dr. Bacon resigned the principalship of the High school. The Board adopted the following :

" *Resolved,* That this Board receives with regret a communication from Dr. Bacon, resigning his position as principal of the High school of Syracuse, N. Y., and

W. K. WICKES.

G. A. LEWIS.

desire to express their thorough appreciation of the
efforts of Dr. Bacon in his position in the High school
during the last ten years, and we extend to him our
hearty good wishes for his success in the field of his
future labors."

Wm. K. Wickes, from Watertown, N. Y., was appointed to succeed Dr. Bacon at a salary of $2,500.

Miss Mary E. Sykes was offered the position vacated
by Mr. Cummings, but could not accept because of a
previous engagement in the Cook County Normal, and
Geo. F. Lewis from Ogdensburg, was appointed.

Miss Belle Cowles, a teacher in the High school, was
granted leave of absence for the purpose of perfecting
herself in the German language, and her place was supplied by the appointment of Miss Rachel Shevelson.

Miss Sawyer who had just returned from a leave of
absence, took the place vacated by Miss Goldman.

Contrary to the usual custom of the Board, a supply
of singing books, to remain the property of the Board,
were ordered purchased to supply the city schools.

Later in the season a resolution was adopted asking
the Legislature to amend the city charter changing the
term of office of the superintendent of schools from one
year to three years.

There had been a difference in the salary of the
assistants to the principals in the senior schools, and at
the February meeting a resolution was adopted fixing
that salary at $500.

The next term in February opened with full rooms in nearly all the schools and a committee of three from the Board were appointed to look over the city and report where school buildings were most needed and in what way greatest relief could be afforded.

On March 5, 1889, William H. Warner was elected president of the Board. The next order of business was the election of clerk and superintendent for three years. Mr. Smith asked permission to leave the room. An informal ballot was ordered, which resulted in giving seven votes to A. B. Blodgett and three votes for Mr. Smith. Commissioner Schmeer moved that the informal ballot be declared formal, and Mr. Blodgett was elected. Commissioner Von Landberg announced that he cheerfully and cordially offered to Mr. Smith the principalship of Prescott school which had become vacant by the election of Mr. Blodgett, and on motion of Commissioner Schmeer he was appointed. After some hesitation and consultation Mr. Smith accepted and assumed the postion, which he still holds.

The committee appointed by the preceding Board to report where new schools were most needed recommended building new houses in the Ninth and Twelfth Wards, and a ten-room building was ordered built to relieve the Fifth and Ninth Wards, and a four-room building for the relief of the Madison school in the Fourteenth Ward. For these purposes an appropriation of $30,000 was made. Lots were purchased and plans and

WILLIAM H. WARNER.

specifications were adopted. A new lot was also purchased in the Fifth Ward, at a cost of $3,500 for enlarging the Grace school-house.

The Board asked to be relieved from repairs on streets, sidewalks, sewers, etc., where appropriations for such purposes had not been asked, and the matter was referred to the city attorney. His decision was that the Common Council should pay for all such expenditures, they being custodians of all city property.

The musical director asked for the purchase of additional charts and other material needed in that department, and also that members of the training class be required to perfect themselves in this branch, as in others, before being granted a diploma for teaching. These requests were approved and carried out, and better facilities for the training class in all departments were secured.

In May, at the suggestion of the superintendent, an appropriation of $200 was made by the Board, and Principals A. E. Kinne and Edward Smith were requested to prepare for publication a history of the city schools. This work was commenced during the summer vacation, but it required too much time and labor to be completed within the year, especially by those engaged in teaching. The work thus begun, however, has resulted in the present volume.

During the autumn of 1889, John W. Smith, connected with the Solvay Process Works, presented a plan for teaching architectural and mechanical drawing in an evening school, volunteering his services, provided the Board of Education would secure suitable room, light, etc. This proposition was gladly accepted. The superintendent acted with Mr. Smith in making necessary provision for the work. This was the beginning of a school which has now been in operation three years, having had more applicants than could be accomodated.

Near the close of the year, the death of Commissioner Thomas Meagher and of the wife of Commissioner Von Landberg brought sorrow into their households, and appropriate resolutions of sympathy and condolence were passed by the Board in each of these cases.

A special meeting of the Board of Education was called to take action on the death of Ansel E. Kinne, principal of Madison school, and appropriate resolutions acknowledging his faithfulness and efficiency as an instructor were passed.

Owing to the exhaustion of the fund appropriated for teachers' wages, an application for opening evening schools was denied.

Early in the fall and winter a sentiment pervaded our city, as it did the State, in favor of placing the American flag upon the school buildings. Through the contributions of the pupils and teachers, nearly all the school-houses were provided with the national emblem.

The new school building in the Ninth Ward was completed and occupied in February, 1890, with Miss Mary

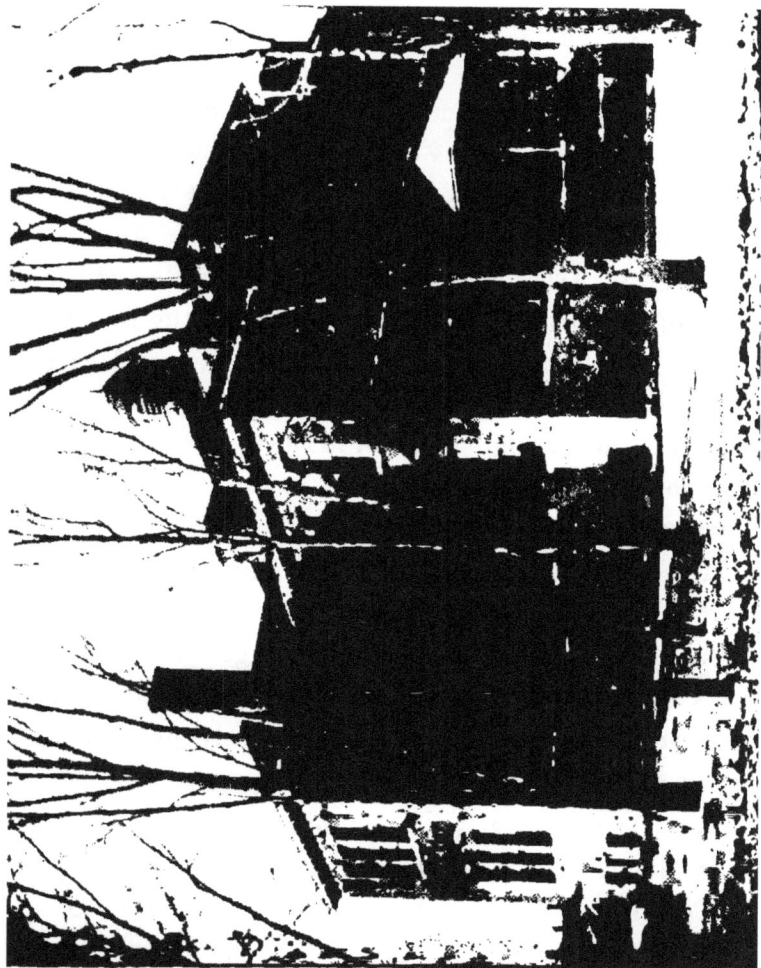

DELAWARE SCHOOL.

W. Flanagan principal. This was a ten-room building, modeled after the Frazer school, in the Third Ward, and cost, including the lot, $23,000. It was not fully completed till the following year, when it was named the Delaware school.

In March, 1890, William Spaulding was elected president of the Board. After the opening of the Delaware school last year, sufficient room had been provided for all the pupils in that part of the city, and what was known as the Magnolia school, in the Geddes annex, was abandoned, the pupils being sent to the Porter and the Delaware schools.

Miss Dwyre in charge of the training class, having shown her adaptability to the work in this city and being known abroad, was strongly urged to leave the work here, at an advance of salary, to take a similar position in the west, but the Board wisely put her salary at $1,000 to retain her services.

J. F. Cooney, after six years' service as assistant clerk of the Board of Education, resigned, and his brother, P. D. Cooney received the appointment to the position.

Beside the school-house erected on the Merrick tract, in the Fifth Ward, already mentioned, plans for altering and improving Salina school, for an addition to the Clinton school, and for the erection of a new house in the Eleventh Ward were adopted, and except the last named were completed during the current year. The estimated cost of the Eleventh Ward house according

WM. SPAULDING.

to the architect for partial completion was $18,996. The contract was signed and the work commenced, but progressed very slowly for want of sufficient means.

Arrangements were made in the autumn, for opening the mechanical drawing school, organized the preceding year, and three evening schools in different parts of the city, for a term of sixteen weeks, four days in a week, All of these were exclusively for pupils not in the regular day schools, and admittance was conditioned upon the recommendation of the ward commissioner. Tuition was free to such as were admitted, books were furnished, the students in the drawing school providing themselves with necessary materials.

A new stipulation for the appointment of teachers, provided that no permanent appointment shall hereafter be made except after a six months' service which shall prove satisfactory to the principal of the school, the superintendent, and the commissioner of the ward.

The superintendent called the attention of the Board to the fact that no provision had been made for rooms for the Board of Education in the new City Hall, and the president of the Board and Superintendent Blodgett were appointed a committee to consult with the Mayor and Common Council in relation to the matter. This resulted in securing convenient and suitable rooms in the south-east corner of the building, second floor.

In February, 1891, by action of the Board of Education, in connection with the Board of Health, an act was passed, forbidding the registering of any pupil in the public schools without the certificate of the health officer.

In March, 1891, Edward C. Wright was elected president of the Board.

Miss Lucy A. Adams, who had been director of

EMMA J. ASBRAND.

drawing for a term of years, resigned, and was appointed teacher of that branch in the High school, and Miss McLennan, of the Oneonta Normal school, was given charge of drawing in all the schools. On account of ill-health she was forced to decline, when it was offered to Miss Emma J. Asbrand, who has occupied the position for one year. She has already gained the confidence and sympathy of teachers and pupils, and has made marked progress. Miss Amelia Weiskotten was also added to the corps of teachers in the High school.

EDWARD C. WRIGHT.

The graduating exercises, at the close of the term end-
ing January, were
held in the Wieting
Opera House for the
High school, and the
Alhambra for the
Advanced A senior
class. The several
senior schools united
in their exercises.
There is no hall large
enough to accommo-
date the citizens who
always turn out to ex-
ercises of the public
school children, and
both of the halls

AMELIA WEISKOTTEN.

were crowded.

During this year a better organization for the teachers' and training classes had been effected and better
results were accomplished. An addition to the lot
belonging to the Merrick school was purchased, by
which it was greatly improved.

During this year, Hon. J. J. Belden sent a communication to the Common Council offering to erect a structure for a Library and Art building for the benefit of
these departments of public education on condition
that a suitable site be provided by the city.

At a meeting of the Board of Education, Commissioner McAllister presented the following resolution, which was adopted :

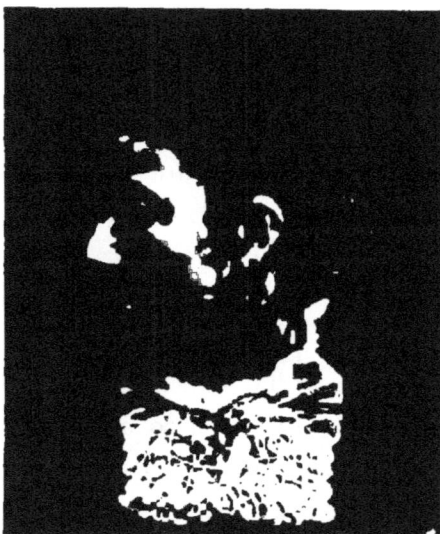

MARY LOUNSBURY,
Principal of Genesee School.

"*Resolved*, That the Board of Education of this city, hereby extends its thanks to the Hon. J. J. Belden for his magnificent and timely gift ; and that we individually pledge him our earnest efforts and best support looking to the fulfillment of his highest wishes and expectations in this grand enterprise."

The Board, by a unanimous vote, gave the free use of the large room in the High school building for the C. L. S. C. university extension course of twelve lectures. This offer was accepted, but popular feeling was so much roused that this room was too small to seat the assembly. The largest city churches were filled to their utmost capacity. A supplementary course was started later in the season when the High school room was occupied and proved satisfactory. By this means two courses, numbering in all twenty-four lectures, were provided to citizens at a nominal price.

At the organization of the Board of Education in March, 1892, Giles H. Stilwell was elected president. New buildings were erected for Montgomery and Grace schools, the perspectives of which here given will illustrate the present ideals of Syracuse in school architecture. In general it may be said that never were our schools more prosperous, our teachers more united, or our system of public education more firmly entrenched in the hearts of the people.

GRACE SCHOOL.

MONTGOMERY SCHOOL

SYRACUSE NY

MERRICK & RANDALL ARCHTS.

The public library has been an important factor in the educational interests of our city and we give a brief history of its organization and growth.

In 1827, Governor Dewitt Clinton recommended the establishment of small libraries in the several district schools of the State. There were about 8,000 of them at that time and 430,000 pupils. The cost of these schools was about $200,000. The suggestion culminated in an act which was passed in 1835, authorizing the purchase of district libraries for the schools of the State.

Previous to this act James Wadsworth, with others, had, in 1831, secured the reprinting and distribution of "Hall's Lectures on School Keeping" to all districts in the State. This was well received and was read by teachers and parents.

Gen. Dix, who was the Secretary of State and ex-officio State Superintendent, was intrusted with the execution of a law giving $55,000 to the several districts, on condition that an equal amount should be raised by them. This met with favor and was heartily responded to throughout the State.

General Dix's successor in 1841 reported the number of volumes in the district libraries to be 422,459, and in 1842, 630,125, an increase in one year of over 200,000 volumes. In 1843 another act was passed permitting the money to be used for the purchase of apparatus and another afterward for the payment of teachers' wages, provided the district contained over fifty children, from five to sixteen years of age, and the library 125 volumes. The superintendent's report this year showed 1,604,210 volumes. Eight years after, in 1861, the report showed a decline, there being only 1,286,536 volumes, a decrease of 317,674 volumes, although the $55,000 had been annually appropriated. The next year the superintendent found the libraries represented by a motley collection of 1,500,000 volumes scattered among the families of the district and piled upon their shelves, or stored away in damp cellars. The Legislature, in 1864, authorized all districts receiving less than $3 to use the money for the payment of teachers' wages or for the purchase of apparatus. The division of library money caused a decline as Superintendent Morgan predicted in 1840.

The Central Library, now, and since its organization, has been under the charge of the Board of Education. The foundation of this library was the district school libraries of the town of Salina, which came into the city under the charter of incorporation. These several libraries were like others heretofore mentioned, a mot-

ley collection of books : some excellent, others worth-
less. The same books were found in many if not in all
the ten districts, and an effort was made by the Board,
in 1857, to avoid duplicating books, and thereby,
with the same expenditure of money, purchase a greater
variety. The libraries of the schools near the centre
of the city were collected at the City Hall, in a room
provided for that purpose, and the books of reference
in all other schools were also brought there. The more
distant schools kept only such books as children would
want to read.

In 1858, all the libraries were placed under the
control of the librarian, and different days assigned for
the several wards to draw books under his direction. This
was soon followed by bringing all the books together at
the Central Library, and fixing certain days of the week
for the several schools to draw. Rooms at the north end
of the old City Hall were arranged with shelving and
book-cases, convenient and attractive.

Under Sec. 19, Chap. 2, of the Rules of the Board,
published in 1857, the superintendent is made " the
librarian, under the direction of the library committee,
and was given charge of the central and district libraries ; to devise some system for the letting, care and
preservation of the books ; and to report to the Board
once a year, the condition and necessities."

The next year, John J. Peck was made chairman of
the library committee and did most excellent work. In

an elaborate report, he said : " The Board fully appreciating the importance of reference and circulating libraries as aids in the great work of education, manifested a desire to raise the standard, by enlarging the libraries and improving them by bringing them within the reach of citizens." That report resulted in the establishment, by consolidation and purchase, of the Central Library, containing 3,000 volumes of standard works. A course of free lectures, partly to stimulate interest in the library, was delivered by several of the citizens in 1857, '58, '59. The library in 1861, contained 3,500 volumes, besides several hundred duplicates, with an average weekly circulation of 500 ; or over 25,000 for the year.

The design at the beginning was : 1st. To make it as complete as possible in the standard and common works upon history, biography, science, etc. 2d. To obtain a large amount of valuable works of reference, books beyond the reach of ordinary readers. 3d. To furnish the best standard works of light literature and a great assortment of juvenile reading.

As the library increased in its usefulness and its circulation, it became necessary to have the librarian always at his post ; and in 1862, John Strachan was made assistant under the direction of the superintendent of schools. He was followed by Patrick McCarthy, who began his official work in March, 1863.

The first published report appeared in 1868, in the

report of the Board of Education, in which is given the number of volumes in 1867 to be 5,227, which was increased in 1868 to 5,870. The circulation was increased more than one hundred per cent in five years. Six hundred seventy volumes had been added by purchase and twenty volumes had been donated during the year. The circulation was over 30,000.

In the report for 1869, 1,373 volumes were added by purchase, and one hundred forty-six by donation. Among those donated were the *London Builder*, containing twenty-five volumes, and fifty-one volumes of the *London Illustrated News*, from 1841 to 1867, given by Andrew D. and Barrett R. White, as before noted.

The Central Library was moved from its too limited quarters in the City Hall building, April 19, 1869, to the High school building; and contained 10,000 volumes. There had been added by purchase 2,472 volumes, and by donation 187 volumes. The circulation the first year after removal averaged 130 a day.

During the following year, Mr. McCarthy died, after seven years of service, and his son William, who had been his assistant for six years, received the appointment, and served three years. John S. Clark succeeded William McCarthy, and served three years. During these six years, the number of volumes increased from 10,592 to 14,070. The average daily loan for this period was more than 133 per day for all days in which the library had been opened to the public.

In the summer of 1875, the bust of the Rev. Samuel J. May was placed in the middle alcove, as before stated.

Mrs. Mary A. Gambia succeeded Mr. Clark as librarian, in 1876, and continued to March, 1879. At the close of her term there were 13,344 volumes in the library, showing a decrease in three years of 726 volumes. The daily loans had averaged 164, and the number of volumes loaned the last year was 47,760.

The Rev. Mr. Mundy, the present librarian, was appointed in 1880. He says :

"The library has doubled in size, and has improved greatly in the quality of its books. The library now contains over 23,000 volumes. During the last few years special attention has been given to the works of reference and to local history. The local history of New York, New Jersey, Pennsylvania, and New England is becoming fairly well presented on the library shelves. The library is moderately good also in general history and poetry. The funds for the use of the library are meagre and the purchases are therefore limited. The popular demand for fiction is such that a large proportion of the money spent has been put into books which are of but temporary value. It is however to the credit of the reading public that while the quality of the books bought during the last ten years has been very much improved, the circulation has increased.

The library is becoming very much cramped in its present place and greatly needs larger rooms. One of our public spirited citizens has undertaken to provide for this need. The Hon. J. J. Belden has offered to erect a library building to cost not less than $150,000. The Common Council has accepted his offer and complied with the conditions named. The people may therefore look forward to see a building for their library which will be an ornament to the city. With this will doubtless come increase of funds for purchasing books. And a few years of judicious management of a small fund for the increase of books will give our library fair standing among the libraries of the Empire State."

MEMBERS AND OFFICERS OF THE BOARD OF EDUCATION

1848.—(1) Wm. Clark, John P. Babcock ; (2) James Noxon, C. M. Brosnan ; (3) HIRAM PUTNAM, Daniel Bradley ; (4) Oliver Teal (till resignation, April 24 ; then T. B. Fitch), Charles A. Wheaton ; *A. G. Salisbury.*

1849.—(1) Wm. Clark (till resignation ; then Mr. Nathan, and afterward John McCarthy), Wm. H. Hoyt; (2) James Noxon, Ira A. Thurber ; (3) HIRAM PUTNAM, Robert R. Raymond ; (4) T. B. Fitch (till resignation in May ; then Smith Ostrum), P. C. Samson ; *A. G. Salisbury* (till resignation ; then *William L. Crandall*).

1850.—(1) William H. Hoyt, John McCarthy ; (2) Ira A. Thurber, John Wilkinson ; (3) Robert R. Raymond (till resignation.; then C. F. Williston), HIRAM PUTNAM ; (4) P. C. Samsom, Charles A. Wheaton ; *William L. Crandall* (till resignation ; then *A. G. Salisbury*).

GILES H. STILWELL.

President of the Board of Education, 1892-93.

1851.—(1) Charles B. Scott, John McCarthy; (2) James C. Hanchett (till resignation; then Alanson Thorp), John Wilkinson; (3) HIRAM PUTNAM, William Bliss Ashley; (4) Charles A. Wheaton, E. T. Hayden; *A. G. Salisbury* (till resignation; then *E. A. Sheldon*).

1852.—(1) Charles B. Scott, James Lynch; (2) John B. Burnett, Alanson Thorp; (3) Wm. Bliss Ashley, Lewis J. Gillett; (4) E. T. Hayden, CHARLES A. WHEATON; *E. A. Sheldon.*

1853.—(1) James Lynch, Matthew Murphy; (2) John B. Burnett, Q. A. Johnson; (3) Lewis J. Gillett (till resignation; then Ansel E. Kinne), William Hall; (4) CHARLES A. WHEATON, E. T. Hayden; *E. A. Sheldon* (till resignation; then *William Hall*).

1854.—The city had been divided into eight wards, and two commissioners from each, increased the Board of Education to sixteen members. (1) John McCarthy, Wm. F. Gere; (2) Walter C. Hopkins, Matthew Murphy; (3) P. S. Stoddard, Q. A. Johnson; (4) N. F. GRAVES, J. G. Wynkoop; (5) H. L. Dinmore (till resignation; then LeRoy Morgan), Ansel E. Kinne (till resignation; then G. H. Hulen); (6) William Bliss Ashley, William Hall; (7) H. D. Hatch, E. T. Hayden (till resignation; then J. A. Allen); (8) W. H. H. Smith, George Barney; *M. L. Brown.*

1855.—(1) John McCarthy, Abram Davis; (2) Matthew Murphy, Christian Freeoff; (3) P. S. Stoddard, Smith Trowbridge; (4) N. F. GRAVES, E. P. Hopkins;

P. J. CODY.   FRANK HOPKINS.

J. J. KEEFE.   P. R. KIELEY.

BOARD OF EDUCATION, 1892-93.

(5) LeRoy Morgan, N. H. Kinne ; (6) Wm. Bliss Ashley, William Hall ; (7) H. D. Hatch, Joseph A. Allen; (8) W. H. H. Smith, W. E. Rose ; *Geo. L. Farnham.*

1856.—(1) Nicholas Cooney, John McCarthy ; (2) Jacob Brand, Matthew Murphy; (3) Smith Trowbridge, Q. A. Johnson ; (4) Edwin P. Hopkins, William J. Hough ; (5) LeRoy Morgan, N. Hildreth Kinne ; (6) William Hall, Francis H. Williams ; (7) Joseph A. Allen, Joseph I. Bradley ; (8) Wm. E. Rose, George J. Gardner ; *Geo. L. Farnham.*

1857.—By another amendment to the city charter each ward will now be represented by one commissioner after another year, when the time for which four of the present Board here elected has expired. (1) N. M. Childs, Nicholas Cooney ; (2) Jacob Brand ; (3) Joseph P. Calanan (died before taking his seat ; then Wm. V. Bruyn) ; (4) Wm. J. Hough ; (5) N. H. Kinne, W. W. Willard ; (6) F. H. Williams (till resignation ; then R. F. Stevens) ; (7) Joseph A. Allen, Joseph I. Bradley ; (8) Geo. J. Gardner ; *Geo. L. Farnham.*

1858.—(1) N. M. Childs; (2) C. M. Henderson; (3) Wm. V. Bruyn ; (4) John J. Peck ; (5) Wm. W. Willard ; (6) R. F. Stevens ; (7) Joseph A. Allen ; (8) C. L. Chandler ; *Geo. L. Farnham.*

1859.—(1) Michael E. Lynch ; (2) C. M. Henderson; (3) Lyman W. Conkey ; (4) John J. Peck ; (5) Titus J. Fenn ; (6) R. F. Stevens ; (7) Joseph A. Allen ; (8) Calvin B. Gay ; *Geo. L. Farnham.*

LeRoy Morgan.
President of the Board of Education, 1856–57.

1860.—(1) Michael E. Lynch ; (2) Jacob Miller ; (3) Lyman W. Conkey ; (4) JOHN J. PECK ; (5) Titus J. Fenn ; (6) Richard F. Stevens ; (7) Joseph A. Allen (resigned, February 19, 1861, after six years of service); (8) Calvin B. Gay ; *Geo. L. Farnham.*

1861.—(1) Walter M. Dallman ; (2) Jacob Miller ; (3) Lyman W. Conkey ; (4) JOHN J. PECK ; (5) Titus J. Fenn ; (6) Richard F. Stevens ; (7) Charles D. Davis ; (8) Calvin B. Gay ; *Geo. L. Farnham.*

1862.—(1) Walter M. Dallman ; (2) Leonard Saxer ; (3) LYMAN W. CONKEY ; (4) Grove L. Johnson ; (5) Titus J. Fenn ; (6) Jas. S. Leach ; (7) Charles D. Davis ; (8) George J. Gardner ; *Geo. L. Farnham.*

1863.—(1) Michael Murray ; (2) Leonard Saxer ; (3) SAMUEL L. COMSTOCK ; (4) Grove L. Johnson ; (5) Arthur H. Wellington ; (6) James S. Leach ; (7) John Hoye ; (8) Geo. J. Gardner ; *Charles E. Stevens.*

1864.—(1) Michael Murray ; (2) Robert Shumann ; (3) SAMUEL L. COMSTOCK ; (4) Samuel J. May ; (5) Arthur H. Wellington ; (6) Nathaniel B. Smith ; (7) John Hoye ; (8) Manning C. Palmer ; *Charles E. Stevens.*

1865.—(1) John O. S. Lynch; (2) Robert Schumann; (3) Samuel L. Comstock ; (4) SAMUEL J. MAY ; (5) Richard E. Lusk ; (6) Nathaniel B. Smith ; (7) Stiles M. Rust ; (8) Manning C. Palmer ; *Charles E. Stevens,* clerk ; *John H. French,* superintendent (till resignation ; then *Charles E. Stevens).*

JAMES McALLISTER.

JOHN A. MACKEY.

JAMES H. MEAGHER.

JOHN J. MOORE, M.D.

BOARD OF EDUCATION, 1892-93.

1866.—(1) John O. S. Lynch ; (2) Thomas J. Leach; (3) Samuel L. Comstock ; (4) SAMUEL J. MAY; (5) Richard E. Lusk ; (6) Orrin Welch ; (7) Stiles M. Rust; (8) John D. Bridges ; *Edward Smith.*

1867.—(1) Thomas Power ; (2) Thomas J. Leach ; (3) John W. Barker; (4) SAMUEL J. MAY; (5) John J. Lynch ; (6) Orrin Welch ; (7) Stiles M. Rust ; (8) John D. Bridges ; *Edward Smith.*

1868.—(1) Thomas Power; (2) John L. Roehner ; (3) John W. Barker ; (4) SAMUEL J. MAY ; (5) John J. Lynch ; (6) Orrin Welch ; (7) Stiles M. Rust ; (8) John D. Bridges ; *Edward Smith.*

1869.—(1) John McCarthy ; (2) John L. Roehner : (3) John W. Barker ; (4) SAMUEL J. MAY ; (5) Nathaniel B. Smith ; (6) Orrin Welch; (7) Stiles M. Rust ; (8) John D. Bridges ; *Edward Smith.*

1870.—(1) John McCarthy ; (2) John Yorkey ; (3) John W. Barker ; (4) Dudley P. Phelps ; (5) NATHANIEL B. SMITH ; (6) Orrin Welch ; (7) Stiles M. Rust ; (8) Darwin L. Pickard ; *Edward Smith.*

1871.—(1) John McCarthy ; (2) John Yorkey ; (3) John W. Barker ; (4) Dudley P. Phelps ; (5) William A. Duncan ; (6) ORRIN WELCH ; (7) Stiles M. Rust ; (8) Darwin L. Pickard ; *Edward Smith.*

1872.—(1) John McCarthy; (2) Henry C. Allewelt; (3) John W. Barker ; (4) George B. Leonard ; (5) William A. Duncan ; (6) Nathaniel B. Smith ; (7) STILES M. RUST; (8) Darwin L. Pickard ; *Edward Smith.*

GEORGE A. SAWYER.

WARREN D. TALLMAN.

L. A. SAXER, M.D.

IRVIN K. WEBB.

BOARD OF EDUCATION, 1892-93.

1873.—(1) Edward E. Chapman ; (2) Henry C. Alle-welt; (3) John W. Barker; (4) George B. Leonard ; (5) William A. Duncan ; (6) Nathaniel B. Smith ; (7) STILES M. RUST ; (8) Darwin L. Pickard ; *Edward Smith.*

1874.—(1) Edward E. Chapman ; (2) Henry C. Alle-welt ; (3) John W. Barker ; (4) Jacob S. Smith ; (5) William A. Duncan ; (6) ORRIN WELCH; (7) Stiles M. Rust ; (8) John B. Tallman ; *Edward Smith.*

1875.—There were no changes in the Board of Edu-cation except in the Seventh Ward, where John J. Crouse succeeded Stiles M. Rust, who had served ten years in the Board. All other retiring commissioners were re-elected. ORRIN WELCH ; *Edward Smith.*

1876.—(1) Edward E. Chapman ; (2) Peter Knaul; (3) John W. Barker; (4) Jacob S. Smith ; (4) WILLIAM A. DUNCAN ; (6) Hiram R. Olmsted ; (7) Martin A. Knapp; (8) John B. Tallman ; *Edward Smith.*

1877.—All commissioners whose terms of office ex-pired were re-elected, and there was no change in the Board. JOHN W. BARKER ; *Edward Smith.*

1878.—(1) Edward E. Chapman ; (2) Peter Knaul ; (3) JOHN W. BARKER ; (4) Henry E. Warne ; (5) Wm. A. Duncan ; (6) Hiram R. Olmsted ; (7) Martin A. Knapp ; (8) John H. Durston ; *Edward Smith.*

1879.—(1) EDWARD E. CHAPMAN ; (2) Peter Knaul; (3) William Brown Smith ; (4) Henry E. Warne ; (5)

William A. Duncan ; (6) Hiram R. Olmsted ; (7) John M. Strong ; (8) John H. Durston ; *Edward Smith.*

1880.—(1) EDWARD E. CHAPMAN (completed eight years of service in the Board, the last two of which he was president) ; (2) J. Daniel Ackerman ; (3) W. Brown Smith ; (4) George C. Young ; (5) William A. Duncan ; (6) Hiram R. Olmsted ; (7) John M. Strong; (8) John H. Durston ; *Edward Smith.*

1881.—(1) Thomas Nicholson ; (2) J. Daniel Ackerman; (3) W. Brown Smith ; (4) George C. Young ; (5) William A. Duncan ; (6) Hiram R. OLMSTED ; (7) John M. Strong; (8) John W. Durston (till resignaton; then D. L. Pickard) ; *E d w a r d Smith.*

CHARES F. WISEHOON, JR.
Member Board of Education. 1892-93.

1882.—Fred W. Willwerth succeeded J. D. Ackerman as commissioner from the Second Ward, all other members remained the same as for the preceding year. HIRAM R. OLMSTED ; *Edward Smith.*

1883.—(1) Michael Maloney ; (2) Fred W. Willworth; (3) W. Brown Smith ; (4) George C. Young ; (5) William A. Duncan ; (6) Hiram R. Olmsted (retired after eight years of service, two of which he was president) ; (7) John T. Jenkins ; (8) Darwin L. Pickard ; *Edward Smith.*

1884.—(1) Michael Maloney ; (2) Daniel Schmeer ; (3) W. Brown Smith (till resignation) ; (4) Alexander Von Landberg ; (5) William A. Duncan ; (6) John W. Yale ; (7) John T. Jenkins; (8) Darwin L. Pickard ; *Edward Smith.*

1885.—(1) Michael Maloney ; (2) Daniel Schmeer ; (3) James M. Belden ; (4) Alexander Von Landberg ; (5) William H. Warner; (6) John W. Yale ; (7) James F. Kennedy ; (8) Darwin L. Pickard (retired from service, having represented his ward eight years on the Board, and two years as president) ; *Edward Smith.*

1886.—(1) Michael Maloney: (2) Daniel Schmeer; (3) James M. Belden ; (4) Alexander Von Landberg ; ·(5) William H. Warner ; (6) Abel C. Benedict; (7) James M. Kennedy ; (8) James B. Brooks ; *Edward Smith.*

1887.—(1) Michael Maloney ; (2) Daniel Schmeer; (3) Thomas Meagher ; (4) Alex. Von Landberg ; (5) William H. Warner ; (6) Abel C. Benedict ; (7) James F. Kennedy ; (8) James B. Brooks ; (9) Edward M. Klock ; (10) Mott R. Pharis ; (11) James R. McAllister ; *Edward Smith.*

1888.—(1) Michael Maloney; (2) Daniel Schmeer; (3) Thomas Meagher; (4) ALEX. VON LANDBERG; (5) William II. Warner; (6) Edward C. Wright; (7) James F. Kennedy; (8) James M. Gilbert; (9) Edward M. Klock; (10) Mott R. Pharis (till resignation; then S. Dempsey); (11) James R. McAllister; *Edward Smith*.

1889.—(1) John Comerford; (2) Daniel Schmeer; (3) Thomas Meagher; (4) Alexander Von Landberg; (5) WILLIAM II. WARNER; (6) Edward C. Wright; (7) William Spaulding; (8) James M. Gilbert; (9) Michael F. Casey; (10) Giles H. Stilwell; (11) James R. McAllister; *A. B. Blodgett*.

1890.—(1) John Comerford; (2) Daniel Schmeer; (3) James II. Meagher; (4) Alex. Von Landberg; (5) William II. Warner; (6) Edward C. Wright; (7) WILLIAM SPAULDING; (8) John A. Tholens; (9) Michael F. Casey; (10) Giles II. Stilwell; (11) James R. McAllister; *A. B. Blodgett*.

1891.—(1) John J. Keefe; (2) Daniel Schmeer; (3) James II. Meagher; (4) Alexander Von Landberg; (5) Warren D. Tallman; (6) EDWARD C. WRIGHT; (7) Patrick R. Kieley; (8) Alexander Grant; (9) Patrick J. Cody; (10) Giles H. Stilwell; (11) James R. McAllister; (12) Charles F. Wisehoon, jr.; (13) John A. Mackay; (14) John A. Tholens; *A. B. Blodgett; P. D. Cooney,* assistant.

1892.—(1) John J. Keefe; (2) Dr. Leonard A. Saxer;

(3) James H. Meagher ; (4) Frank Hopkins ; (5) Warren D. Tallman ; (6) Dr. John J. Moore ; (7) Patrick Kieley ; (8) George C. Sawyer ; (9) Patrick J. Cody ; (10) GILES H. STILWELL ; (11) James R. McAllister ; (12) Charles F. Wischoon, jr.; (13) John A. Mackay ; (14) Irvin K. Webb ; *A. B. Blodgett ; P. D. Cooney,* assistant.

PRESIDENTS OF THE BOARD

Name.	Date.	Years.
Capt. Hiram Putnam,	1848–51,	4
Charles A. Wheaton,	1852–53,	2
Nathan F. Graves,	1854–55.	2
LeRoy Morgan,	1856,	1
William J. Hough,	1857,	1
N. M. Childs,	1858,	1
John J. Peck,	1859–61,	3
Lyman W. Conkey,	1862,	1
Samuel L. Comstock,	1863–64,	2
Samuel J. May,	1865–69,	5
Nathaniel B. Smith,	1870,	1
Orrin Welch,	1871,	1
Stiles M. Rust,	1872–73,	2
Orrin Welch,	1874–75,	2
William A. Duncan,	1876,	1
John W. Barker,	1877–78,	2
Edward E. Chapman,	1879–80,	2
Hiram R. Olmsted,	1881–82,	2
W. Brown Smith,	1883,	1
Darwin L. Pickard,	1884–85,	2
Michael Maloney,	1886–87,	2
Alexander Von Landberg,	1888,	1
William H. Warner,	1889,	1
William Spaulding,	1890,	1
Edward C. Wright,	1891,	1
Giles H. Stilwell,	1892,	

SUPERINTENDENTS OF SCHOOLS

Albert G. Salisbury,	1848–50,	1 yr. 10 mo.
William L. Crandall,	1850,	5 months.
Albert G. Salisbury,	1850–51,	10 months.
Edward A. Sheldon,	1851–53,	2 years.
William Hall,	1853–54,	10 months.
Mortimer L. Brown,	1854–55,	1 year.
George L. Farnham,	1855–63,	8 years.
Charles E. Stevens,	1863–66,	3 years.
Edward Smith,	1866–89,	23 years.
A. Burr Blodgett,	1889–	Now in office.

Jefferson school (No. 3), built 1848 ; enlarged 1874.

Montgomery school (No. 11), built 1851 ; enlarged 1857 ; rebuilt 1892.

Townsend school (No. 12), built 1851 ; enlarged 1861 ; enlarged 1881.

Seymour school (No. 9), built 1852 ; enlarged 1862, 1865, 1881 ; rebuilt 1882.

Salina school (No. 8), enlarged 1852, 1858 ; abandoned and new house built 1859, 60 ; enlarged 1871 ; burned and rebuilt 1873 ; remodeled 1890.

Irving school (No. 13), built 1857 ; enlarged 1866 ; rebuilt 1881.

Putnam school (No. 7), enlarged 1857, 1863 ; burned and rebuilt 1871 ; enlarged 1881 ; new house on new lot built 1888.

Clinton school, built 1859 ; enlarged 1861, 1866, 1870.

Genesee school (No. 4), built 1862 ; enlarged 1870.

High school, built 1867, 68.

May school, built 1867 ; remodeled, 1885.

Franklin school, 1869, 70 ; remodeled 1886.

Fayette school (No. 6) and Lodi school (No. 10), abandoned, 1871.

Madison school, built 1871.

Grace school, built 1874 ; rebuilt 1892.

Adams school, built 1874.

Prescott school, enlarged 1867 ; abandoned and new building built 1881.

Frazer school, built 18—; burned and rebuilt 1887.

Vine school, built 1887.

Bassett school, built 1890.

Merrick school, built 1890.

Delaware school, built 1890.

Brighton school, built 1891.

FINANCIAL STATEMENT

	No. of Teachers	Teachers' Wages.	Janitors' Wages.	Library.	Temporary Supplies.	Permanent Fund.	City Appropriation.	State Appropriation.	Regents' Appropriation.
1848	24	$ 7,602.48	$ 99.57	$ 179.36	$ 650.19	$ 3,000.00	$ 8,818.00	$ 1,357.19	$
1849	25	6,120.29	159.43	574.06	3,719.90	4,997.28	8,208.98	2,186.02	
1850	28	7,134.50	206.56	625.86	3,320.13	681.00	8,247.00	4,211.57	
1851	32	8,340.85	246.94	558.30	677.57	4,544.42	8,247.00	5,654.64	
1852	38	10,333.43	290.50	745.60	4,067.58	2,768.24	12,000.00	5,500.00	
1853	43	10,310.07	307.25	559.30	3,982.25	3,664.64	15,140.47	5,727.11	
1854	46	8,520.39	426.65	589.60	4,238.74	924.25	13,733.17	5,768.49	
1855	50	15,119.41	600.00	625.46	4,400.00	None.	15,395.46	5,414.41	
1856	49	15,198.62	737.93	801.10	5,373.02	2,520.28	17,000.00	5,847.98	
1857	54	15,649.28	856.30	647.93	8,333.77	7,904.66	19,185.59	8,615.72	
1858	57	19,247.17	1,127.75	848.84	6,657.64	5,852.61	18,531.48	9,224.68	
1859	64	19,857.27	1,441.90	719.27	6,000.51	6,150.46	24,185.98	8,615.72	
1860	74	21,906.04	1,460.79	1,043.02	422.09	6,980.05	21,272.73	8,226.84	
1861	80	21,755.00	1,477.55	845.79	5,929.77		19,949.85	9,038.87	% 278.60
1862	88	22,083.91	1,563.57	418.49	6,878.15	5,000.00	20,848.84	9,283.00	
1863	95	23,481.38	1,704.11	623.67	9,583.50	8,418.10	31,550.20	9,424.77	
1864	103	28,336.47	1,886.75	905.73	1,371.27	5,809.08	37,817.60	9,439.00	
1865	115	35,693.52	2,364.75	814.15	14,066.46	3,448.38	64,112.55	11,044.46	
1866	120	38,321.05	2,384.65	1,554.58	15,737.45	8,311.53	56,112.55	11,044.46	
1867	133	48,871.45	3,410.35	2,599.94	13,914.64	10,211.13*	58,049.45	11,609.89	143.07
1868	153	56,449.46	3,926.00	4,211.01	23,523.40	23,003.07†	70,900.00	19,212.19	273,48
1869	170	68,734.47	5,023.93	7,090.50	28,880.34	29,230.22‡	113,900.00	20,620.41	320,70

Year									
1870	173	73,765.90	5,367.38	4,671.92	29,367.43	25,945.23½	113,800.00	21,008.08	573.06
1871	174	79,271.23	5,764.15	5,100.27	36,516.09	24,745.73	119,600.00	22,879.60	1,223.63
1872	179	85,083.69	6,145.72	3,778.41	30,557.25	35,880.13	99,000.00	26,384.85	1,121·64
1873	182	88,014.14	6,159.45	3,634.75	29,525.73	1,446.90	100,000.00	26,309.98	5,009.24
1874	199	93,341.81	6,397.60	4,086.36	30,251.92	22,166.54	120,000.00	26,294.79	4,295.97
1875	207	97,279.61	6,562.98	3,162.75	24,155.45	23,912.22	116,000.00	27,212.07	1,157.46
1876	173	94,706.65	6,051.00	3,240.50	21,488.50	4,774.88	96,200.00	30,714.25	1,506.87
1877	172	82,651.37	5,693.84	3,566.30	17,567.76	1,017.50	75,000.00	31,537.84	1,451.58
1878	177	79,337.09	5,479.79	3,308.95	18,470.45	2,500.00	75,000.00	31,467.47	1,527.09
1879	179	81,498.60	5,479.29	1,773.05	15,746.62		72,500.00	29,159.53	1,498.71
1880	183	85,552.87	5,569.04	2,079.77	14,135.39	22,500.00	75,000.00	29,601.32	1,354.36
1881	191	84,332.43	5,360.04	2,653.51	18,020.71	18,272.10	93,900.00	29,489.95	1,289.05
1882	183	90,994.43	5,828.04	2,728.32	22,608.57	20,265.26	90,000.00	29,569.51	1,400.00
1883	186	97,528.45	5,897.61	3,126.87	20,440.59	17,868.38	93,900.00	29,482.95	1,289.05
1884	197	98,713.73	6,232.00	4,000.16	27,036.37		104,868.33	29,431.67	1,294.05
1885	203	102,077.15	6,850.00	3,100.71	25,372.10		106,687.45	29,597.30	1,288.67
1886	200	107,641.11	6,888.89	3,107.09	37,068.34	8,000.00	118,579.31	29,178.94	1,520.06
1887	264	137,464.08	9,921.79	3,057.31	37,713.24	18,497.86	141,566.69	41,642.26	3,292.88
1888	275	147,081.79	9,321.95	5,487.16	35,915.97	39,723.11	157,611.04	38,096.15	3,068.96
1889	284	132,702.10	10,249.28	5,298.65	38,043.28	25,140.21	155,296.72	43,693.67	2,946.53
1890	288	157,851.85	10,877.28	3,500.00	34,082.93	32,424.36	160,390.44	41,281.48	3,102.30
1891	298	167,596.73	11,563.58	3,850.00	39,433.55	25,284.19	165,098.23	48,424.17	3,138.92
1892									

* Not including $30,496.18 on High school.

† Including $17,644.10 for May school.

‡ Including $23,620.87 for High school.

§ Including $13,400.00 for Franklin school.

SAMANTHA LINCOLN,
Montgomery.

MRS. L. E THOMAS,
Brighton.

ELIZA G. CHAPMAN,
Irving.

MRS. MARY A. VAN ANTWERP,
May.

PRINCIPALS OF JUNIOR SCHOOLS.

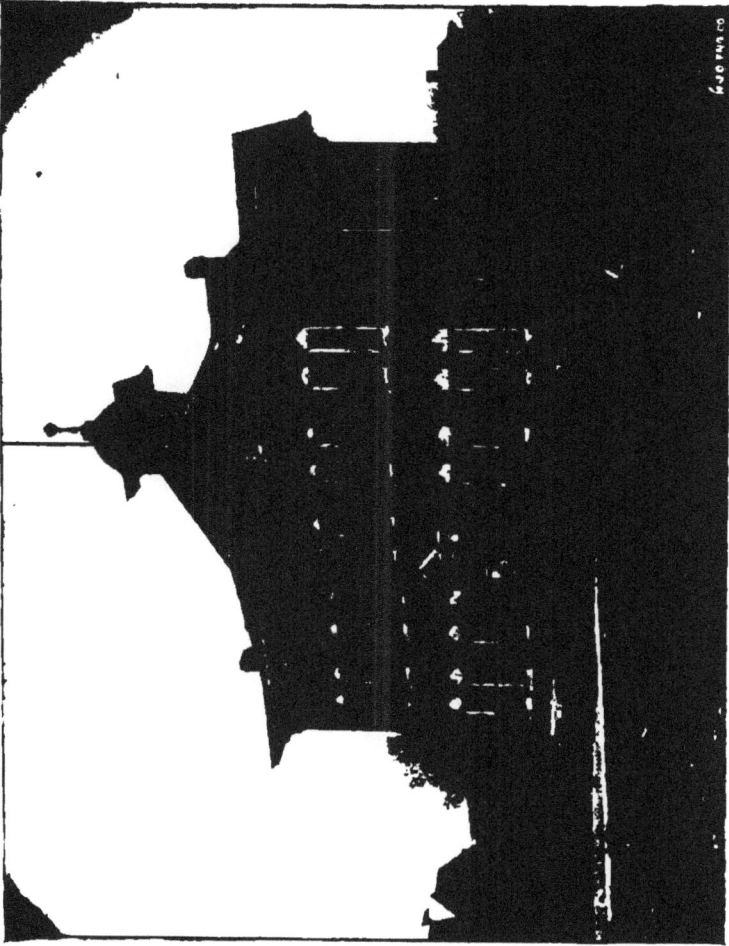

DANFORTH SCHOOL.

ALPHABETICAL LIST OF TEACHERS

With date of appointment, years of service, and schools where employed, designated by letters.

NOTE.—a, High; b, Salina; c, Jefferson; d, Townsend; e, Franklin; f, Genesee; g, Frazer; h, Prescott; i, Clinton ; j, Vine ; k, Fayette ; l, Seymour ; m, May; n, Grace; o, Montgomery; p, Putnam ; q, Irving ; r, Lodi ; s, Madison ; t, Delaware ; u. Porter ; v, Gere ; w, Magnolia; x, Danforth; y, Brighton; z. Rose; A, Adams; B, Bassett; aa, Onondaga Orphan Asylum; bb, St. Vincent de Paul's Orphan Asylum; nn, Merrick ; *, now teaching ; †, Portrait; Dec., Deceased; W. sch., Winter school. In dates, the 1800 is omitted.

Abbott, Harriet E.; 54-69; b, c; Syr.

Abbott, Nellie J.; 72; Mrs. John Duncan, Syracuse.

Abbott, Nellie S.; 88-92; s, y, *

Abel, Nettie S.; 77 ; l.

Ackerman, Mattie B.; 89-92; p, *

Adams, Maria E.; 65-76; f, n, o, q, s, Michigan.

Adams, Isabel H.; 62-68; q.

Adams, Lucy A.; 67-92; a, f, *, †.

Adams, Marcia ; 52-53; q.

Adams, Sophia ; 53-55; s.

Adams, John Q.; 81-92 ; x, y, * †

Alden, Nellie M.; 72-74; q, Mrs. Coit.

Allen, Caverno D.; 48-50; a, f, went to Rome, N. Y.

Allen, Sophia; 53-55; a, s, married.

Allin, Mrs. Maria; 52-53; s.

Aldrich, Albina; 75-80; n. Detroit, Michigan.

Allis, James A., 70-80; w. sch. Syr.

Allis, Carrie L.; 84-91; e; Syr.

Allis, Mary D.; 88-90; a, Syr.

Anabel, Miss; 75; u. Mrs. Henry Smith, Syr.

Anderson, Frances; 54-74; s, Syr.

Arnold, Sarah M.; 58-92; a, o, *; Syr.

Arnold, Wealthy; 68; o, deceased.

Arnold, Emma E.; 71; a.

Arnold, Mattie; 71-77; o.

Arnold, Mary; 88-90; b, Mrs. George Hubbs, Syr.

Arnzt, Caroline M.; 68-76; e. Mrs. Cushney, widow, California.

Ashfield, Elizabeth; 58-61; q, Mrs. Thomas Lunn, widow, Syr.

(269)

LAURA M. GEARY,
Gere.

ABBIE ISAACS,
Vine.

HARRIET E. ABBOTT,
Jefferson (formerly).

MISS FLANAGAN,
Delaware.

PRINCIPALS OF JUNIOR SCHOOLS.

Austin, Mrs. Alice; 65; l, Mrs. Swan, Brooklyn.

Averel, Frances; 55; u.

Avery, Miss E. C.; 68; o.

Avery, Jennie A.; 70-72; a.

Avery, Mrs. H. S.; 61; o.

Avery, Mrs. Marietta S.; 56-60; o.

Avery, Harriet; 60-64.

Ayers, Daniel ; 73 ; b.; Syr.

Babcock, Lucy E.; 70-73; m, s; Mrs. C. W. Smith.

Babcock, Agnes E.; 72-77; m, s; Mrs. Wood, Syracuse.

Bacon, George A.; 74-89; a; Allen & Bacon, Boston, Mass.

Bach, Lottie E.; 78-92; e, *

Bailey, B. N.; 72, 73 ; w. sch.

Bailey, William; 48; u.

Bailey, Leon O.; 78; u, x.

Baker, Mary; 68-92; p, m, n, *

Baker, Adella L.; 75-92; m, *

Bakeman, B. L.; 78; w. sch.

Balger, Etta; 91, 92; n, *

Baldwin, Clara ; 54-56; k, m, p.

Baldwin, Charles G.; 72, 73 ; w. sch.

Baldwin, Ellen; 66-92; l, m, q, s, *

Ball, Carrie; 62; d.

Ballou, E. F.; 72-76; music.

Bainbridge, Anna E.; 86-92; b, o. *

Bainbridge, Lizzie ; b ; Mrs. ——, California.

Banister, Mary E.; 73-86; a, l, q; Syr.

Barker, Phoebe; s.

Barker, Amelia, 48-50; v.

Barker, F. W.; 81 ; x.

Barnum, Gen. Henry A.; 52, 59 ; b ; died, 1890.

Barber, Alice; 62-64; l.

Barber, Margaret, 67-71 ; m ; Mrs. Horace Kendall, Syr.

Bardwell, Louise; 70, 71; p.

Barron Mrs. Eva L. (Williams) ; 73-78; b, l, *; Kentucky.

Barnes, Lilian C.; 83-86; o; married.

Barrett, H. E. (Pr.); 80-92; b, c, * †

Barrett, Margaret, 86-92; u, *

Barney, Mary A.; 75-90; l, p, m ; Meadville, Pa.

Barnes, J. H.; 50 ; u.

Barry, Ellen E.; 79-92; p, *

Bassett, Minerva M.; 68-70 ; q ; Mrs. J. Will Page, Syr.

Bassett, Mary A.; 60-62; p, q ; Mrs. Davis, New York City.

Bateson, Rose; 63; p.

Bates, Ella; 63, 64; k, m; Mrs. Miner, died 1872.

Baum, Mary; 49; s.

Baumgrass, Augusta C.; 87-92; e, *

Barnes, J. H.; 50; u.

Beal, J. B.; 48; (Pr) p, u.

Beach, Fanny; 64-67; l.

Beach, Ada M.; 74-83; A; Mrs. Chas. Smith, Syr.

Bailey, William; 48; u.

Beebe, Charlotte; 51.

Beebe, Harriet; 63-66; r ; Mrs. William Greenland, Syr.

Becker, Miss; (Pub) 72; w; Mrs. Robert Gere, Syr.

Beebe, Hattie; 64-66; i, s, Syr.

Beebe, Mary S.; 64-67; d, h; dec.

Beebe, Mattie; 64-65; o.

Beebe, Florence; 54-57; m.

Behan, Margaret F.; 78-92; b. *

Belknap, Samuel L.; 68, 75, 77; w. sch.

Brinkerhoff, Sarah: 72-81; Mrs. Amidon, Marcellus, N. Y.

Brown, Mortimer L.; 53,54; c; † died, 1888.

Brown, Perez ; 54-56 ; a, f.

Brown, Ellen ; 56 ; o.

Brown, Harriet E.; 51-53; r.

Brown, Mrs. Libbie (Palmer) ; 61-92; l, * †

Brownell, W. A.; 71-92 ; a. * †

Brownell, Alice J·; 75-89; h, i. *; Denver, Colo.

Brooks, Miss J. B.; 48; p; Mrs. Castle, Geneva, O.

Brooks, Sarah M.; 56-57; p.

Brooks, Charlotte J.; 56, 57; d.

Bruegel, N. Roberta; 89-92 ; h, *

Buck, Ellen A.; 68-70; q.

Buckley, Ellen.

Buler, Florina; 92; A. *

Bunnell, Emma F.; 71-78; p, A; Mrs. Rupert, Geneva, N. Y.

Bunnell, Fanny S.

Burgess, Mrs. Jennie L.; 62-69 ; d, f, h.

Burdick, Hattie R.; 62-70; l, o.

Burdick, Isaac E.; 71-80; h; went to Chattanooga, Tenn.

Burdick, Nettie A.; 68-71; k, l; Mrs. Allen Sharpley, Oakland, Cal.

Burdick, Louise; 78; married.

Burch, Mary E.: 58-60; h, u; dec.

Burrill, Maria; 58, 59; u.

Burk, Mary; 58-86; d,p,A; died 1886, Syr.

Buckley, Ellen: 91-92; u. *

Burritt, Fanny; 75; c; Mrs. Miles Syencer, Syr.

Burnett, Sarah; 53-60; k, p; dec.

Burnham, Sarah P.; 54, 55; b.

Burnett, Frances; 54—; b.

Burt, Hattie C.; 70-75; d; dec.

Buss, Laura M.; 91-92; h. *

Bushnell, Marion E.; 63-92; p, s, * †

Butler, Ebenezer; 64, 66-73, 82-87; l, u, x; † Syr.

Burroughs, Phoebe J.; 57-61; h, m.

Butts, Angeline; 49, 50; p.

Byrne, Mary F.; 85-92; p. A. *

Cady, Mary; 54; u.

Caldwell, Genevieve A.; 69, 70; m, q; dec.

Calthrop, Edith; 91,92; y.

Cameron, A. G.; 72, 73; u.

Cameron, L. May; 79-92; n, nn. *

Camp, Theodore D.; 64 67; p, * N. York City.

Campbell, Joanna M.; 74-89; a, d. s; New Hartford, N. Y.

Campbell, Gertrude T.: 70; a.

Campbell, Isabel G.; 76-78; s; dec.

Carpenter, Jane A.; 57-61-74; b, o.

Carpenter, Mrs. J. A.; 61-84; f, l, o,p;

Carter, Ellen; 70.

Caraher, Catherine M.; 69-86; d, s; died 1886.

Carroll, Nellie; 89-92; i, *

Carew, Anna; 65-76; i; Mrs. Wm. Benson, Syr.

Carter, Isabel: 68-70; b; Mrs. Marshall Burroughs, Syr.

Case, Miss; 69; u; married.

Casey, Ella; 88, 90; x ; married.

Casey, Elliette W.; 55-58; f; dec.

Casey, Augusta; 60; n.

Castle, Kittie M.; 73-75; l; Seneca Falls.

Coleman, Laura A.; 70-71; l, u; Mrs. Geo. A. Mosher, Syr.

Coleman, Blanche H.; 88, 92; l, *

Collins, Kate M.; 82-92; l, *

Collins, Agnes; 78-90; bb, *

Collins, Grace M.; 83-92; l, *

Cole, Ella A.; 66-75; l,q; married, Syr.

Colwell, Florence (Booth); 68-71; p; Detroit.

Colwell, Fanny; 88-92; c, *

Cole, Sarah A.; 68-69; e.

Conkey, Mrs. Lucy M.; 75-80; d, i, Syr.

Cone, Mary E.; 64, 65; c.

Congdon, C. A.; 76; w. sch.

Cool, Myra E.; 70-75; l,n; Mrs. Alonzo Talmage, New Haven, Conn.

Cook, Wm. H.; 52, 53; l.

Cook, Luvan, 51.

Cook, Winnie (Barber); 68-83; l, m, n; dec., 1883.

Cook, Ella H.; 87-92; q, *

Copeland, Susan J.; 83; Mrs. Ed. Andrews, Syr.

Corey, Angenetta P.; 57-60; l; Mrs. Burdick.

Corey, Sarah A.; 59-67; o, q. s; Mrs. Henry Burdick; now Mrs. Cleveland Orville, Cal.

Corbin, Lucy A.; 55-63; c, d; Mrs. John Wild, Royalton, Vt.

Cornelle, Lewis D.; 48, 49; b, l; died, 1883, Chicago, Ill.

Corwin, Angenetta; 57-67; o, aa; Syr.

Cornwell, Edith; 91; v.

Cowles, Belle W.; 86-91; a; Mrs. D. Cass Mason, Syr.

Cox, Susan M.; 48; p; Battle Creek, Mich.

Cooper, T.; 47; u.

Crane, Josie P.; 65-71; d, r, s; dec.

Crawford, Kate; 50-53; p; married.

Crowley, Abby; 67-92; s, *

Crowen, Mary E.; 66-74; d, e, o; Syr.

Cross, Anna; 41; u.

Cowles, Clara L.; 72.

Coykendall, Mary T.; 73-88; u.

Cullen, Mrs. Kate M.; 61-66, 69-92; Prin., c, d, * †

Culver, Addie S.; 60-62; l, o, q.

Cummings, Lizzie E.; 83-92; q *

Cummings, Sarah A.; 89-92; A *

Cummings, Nettie F.; 80-92; nn, n *

Cunningham, Mary, 70-73; bb.

Curtis Julia A. (Hardee); 80-82; c, l.

Daily, Kate; 82-91; l; died, 91.

Daily, Mary; 85-92; l *

Dakin, Libbie M.; 67-72, 73; o, m; Mrs. C. W. Lane.

Dake, Louisa; 63-65; d.

Dashley, Emma E., 87-92; e *

Dann, Mrs. Millie E.; 72-74; l, q, s; Mrs. Dr. Mott, Syr.

Daniels, A. J.; 59; u.

Davis, Harriet L.; 49-56; b, c; Mrs. Thomas, Englewood.

Davis, Helen M.; 61, 62; c; married, Syr.

Davis, Mary E.; 75, 76; i, q.

Davey, Emma; 89-90; o.

Davey, Kate; 62.

Dean, Clara A.; 58-68; b, c, o; went south after the war.

Dee, Anna F.; 86-92; h *

Delano, Mary; 90-92; l *

Delany Rose M.; 89-92; n, t *

Delany, Ella V.; 87-92; l *
Delany. Mary F.; 84-92; n *
Delany, Margaret F.; 88-90; n; Syr.
Dennis, Carrie; g; married; Syr.
Dennison, George B.; 49; p.
Dennison, Mary A.; 50.
DePuy, Mrs. Julia; 66-69; b, i; Syr.
Deveau, Clara A.; 66-68; l; Mrs.
    Russell; dec.
Deveau, F. Adelle; 68-73; b, k, o;
    Mrs. Curtis, widow, Cal.
Deveau, Bridget A.; 90-92; d *
Dewey, Kate; 62; o.   •
Dickie, Ella M.; 69, 70; m; Mrs. Ed.
    Wagoner, Syr.
Dimmock, Lizzie W.; 63-66; b, c, l;
    Mrs. George B. Leonard, Syr.
Dolphin, Anna; 82-86; p, q; Mrs. M.
    Mellon, Buffalo, N. Y.
Dolphin, Anastasia; 84, 85; q.
Donaldson, Anna; 91, 92; u *
Dore, Kate E.; 85-92; b *
Douglass, Belle; 65-92; d, h *
Doud, Mrs.; 74; u.
Dow, Bertha M.; 66-72; o.
Drake. Julia; 68; f; married.
Drake, Louisa;
Driscoll, Michael; 77-78; f; w. sch.
Duffee, Minnie E.; 85-90; l; Mrs. Pat-
    rick Johnson, Syr.
Dupont, Alfonse; 74-76; a.
Dunbar, Debora; 68-92; e, l, m, n, *
Dunham, Luella S.; 72-73; l, m; Pom-
    pey, N. Y.
Dunham, Jennie A.; 75-79; e. i.
Dunford, Honora A.; 85-92; e *
Dunford, Lizzie W.; 83-92; c, b *
Dunford, Minnie T.; 79-87; b; Mrs.
    Patrick Murray, Syr.

Dunn, Margaret A.; 66-78; b; Mrs.
    Farmer, widow, Syr.
Dunn, Mary G.; 67-71; d; Mrs. Grace,
    widow, Syr.
Dunn, Ella M.; 72-73; c; Mrs. M. J.
    Chryst, Syr.
Dunn, Kittie T.; 80-92; b, c *
Dunn, Anna V.; 83-91; h, l, *; teach-
    er of drawing and music, Hor-
    nelsville, N. Y.
Durston, A. S.; 75; w. sch.
Durant, Margaret A.; 60-62; f; dec.
Dwyre, Mary L.; 68-92; k, o, p, *;
    training class.
Dwyre, Lizzie C.; 73-92; o, *
Dwyre, Wm. F.; 78, 79; w. sch.
Dwyre, Kittie L.; 84-92; A, p, *

Earll, Delia N.; 48-55; c; Cal.
Earll, Mary; 53; c.
Earll, Electa L.; 58-80; b,c; died, 1880,
    Baldwinsville.
Eastman, Sylvia J.; 57-65; p, d; Pa.
Eagan, Minnie A.; 87-92; v, *
Ecker, Sarah J.; 61-65; i; dec.; Fay-
    etteville, N. Y.
Edick, P. H.; 78-81; x, *; Rochester.
Ellis, Minnie H.; 62-68; q, p *; Brook-
    lyn, N. Y.
Elmer, Ida M.; 72-75; m; Mrs. Frank
    Enney, Syr.
Emmons, Amanda J.; 65-67; c, f, o;
    Cal.
Emerson, Margaret; 70-92; i. *
Enders, Margaret M.; 87-92; t *
Enny, Ida M.; 75; u.
Enos, D. C.; 45; u.
Ettleson, Etta; 90-92; p *
Ettleson, Dora; 85-87; o.

Evans, Sarah E.; 50; c; Mrs, James Johonnot; N. Jer,

Evans, Ellen A.; 56-63; d, h, k; Mrs. Nelligan, San Francisco.

Evans, Lola M.; 61-67; h, l.

Evans, Donna; 53-55; h, k; Cal.

Eustace, Margaret M.; 84-92; b, c *

Fairchild, Gussie; 78; s.

Fairchild, Kittie R.; 78-82; s; married, Kansas.

Fairchild, Lizzie M.; 74-85; d, m, l; Mrs. Will Gray, Syr.

Farley, Mary; 55-56; u.

Falvy, Alvaretta; 88-92; x, y *

Fancher, Mary J.; 74-75, 77-92; b, f, h, *

Farnham, George L.; 50-51; c; †; Prin. Nebraska Normal school, Peru.

Farnham, Mrs. George L.; 50-51, 57-58; c, d: dec.

Farnham, Abby; 51; b.

Farnham, Elizabeth, 69-71; l; m; Mrs. Buxton, widow, Syr.

Fayler, George W.;

Fenn, Jane; 54, 55; l.

Fisher, Mary E.; 60-92; f, p, s, *

Fitzgerald, Alice E.; 68-78; 84-89; c, i; Mrs. Charles Hanna, Syr.

Finkelstein, Brinna; 88-92; q, s, *

Fix, Cora; g; Mrs. Johnson; Syr.

Flanagan, Mary W.; 86-92; t, * †

Flach, Marie L.; 83-92; e, *

Fleming, Miss; 53; h.

Foote, Charles J.; 69-73; a; dec.

Foote, Mrs. C. J.; 73; a; dec.

Foote, William Y.; 89-92; a, *

Ford, Mary; 75-92; b, c, * †

Ford, Celia; 83-88; c, *; west.

Ford, Louisa; 87-92; h; Mrs. Fred Sloan.

Foster, Marion A.; 74; i; died, 83

Foster, Lizzie A.; 81-92; m, *

Foster, James; 61-62; u.

Fox, Libbie; 70, 71; p.

Freeland, Maria; 60-68; l; Mrs. Chas. Pratt, Dewitt.

Freeman, Estella; 68-73, 77, 85; b, c; Mrs. W. Raney; dec.

Freeland, Sarah; 69-92; l, m. q, *

Freeland, Margaret; 73-92; e, o, i, *

French, Mary; 65.

Frost, Cordelia; 56, 57; f.

Fuller, Libbie M.; 67; s; Syr.

Fuller, Laura E.; 70-73; o, m; Mrs. Warren, Savannah, Ga.

Fuller, Dr.; 87; t.

Fullmer, D. M.; 57; u.

Gage, Mrs. Maud E.; 67-81; Mich.

Gallavin, Mary E.; 91-92; v, *

Gallivan, Mary V.; 91; v.

Garfield, Nellie F,; 87, 88; x; died, 1890.

Gannon, Lizzie M.; 85-91; m; Mrs, M. J. Kennedy; Syr.

Gaylord, Orra M.; 53-59; Mrs. S. Collins, Indianapolis.

Gaylord, Lucetta S.; 54-65; 68-82; q, s, aa; dec.

Gaylord, Louisa R.; 58-61.

Gaylord, Amelia H.; 50-86; p, s, q, aa, died, Syr.

Gaylord, Hester A.; 81-86.

Gaylord, Elizabeth R.; 58-61; s. Indianapolis.

Geary, Laura M.; 80-92; g, v, w, * †

Genett, Miss; 67.

George, Amelia (Chapman); 63-67, 77-80, 83-90; p, q, *.

Gere, Louisa O.; 63-66; f; Mrs. Virgil Price, Flushing, L. I.

Gere, Mary E.; 88-92; f, o; *.

Gilbert, Sarah A.; 60-61, 63-65; b, d; Mrs. Bridgeford; dec.

Gilbert, James M.; 76; w. sch.

Gilbert, Ida V.; 79-88; b, c; Mrs. Jas. Gilbert. Syr.

Gilmore, Mrs. Amelia (Chedzoy); 66-70, 74-78; o; died, 78.

Goldstein, Marilla; 74-84; Mrs. Rabbi Guttmann, Syr.

Goldman, Ida E.; 86, 87; a.

Goodrich, Mrs. Leonora L.; 73-92; h, i, * †

Gooley, Sarah W.; 80-89; v.

Gooley, Ella V.; 83-92; u, v, *

Gould, Emily C.; 55, 56; u.

Gould, Edith M.; 73, 74; l; married.

Gould, Helen E.; 74-92; q, *

Graves, Charlotte E.; 71, 72; h.

Graves, Addie S.; 85-92; u, t, *

Green, Olivia; 53.

Griffith, Olivia; 63-69; d, f, l, m; dec.

Griffith, Nellie E.; 78-81; m; Mrs. Charles Meldram, Syr.

Griffin, Milton J.; 81-86; a; * west.

Griffin, George L.; 72, 73; a; dec.

Groot, Mrs. Anna; 70-71; q.

Grodevant, Mary A.; 49; b.

Hall, Celia A.; 51-58; a, d, h.

Hall, Julia A.; 73-85; q, s; Mrs. Merriman, widow, Cazenovia.

Hall, Catharine N.; 77-92; f, *

Hale, Francis P.; 63, 64; l; Syr.

Hale, Lyda M.; 63-66; o, l.

Hamlin, Flora; 71-92; l, m, *

Hamilton, Ella S.; 69-71; h; Mrs. Hinsdale, now Mrs. A. C. Furgeson, Saratoga.

Hamilton, Grace; 87-92; m, *

Hampton, Gussie M.; 88-92; n, *

Hancock, Emma; 67.

Handright, Mary E.; 85-92; u, *

Handright, Nellie.

Hanley, Sarah T.; 90-92; d, x, *

Hanley, Nellie A.

Hardendorf, Ida A.; 75-80; l, m; dec.

Handrahan, Nellie A.; 84-92; v, *

Hapgood, Kittie E.; 67-78; s; Brooklyn, N. Y.

Harris, Mrs. Maria W.; 65-72; a; Homer, N. Y.

Harris, Geo. N.; 49-62; b, k, l; died, 85

Harris, Mrs. Geo. N.; 50-59; k; widow, Syr.

Harris, Ada A.; 80-92; l, *

Harmon, Mrs. Marietta; 83-92; p, q, *

Harlow, Wm.; 80-82; a, * †

Hartnet, Josephine, 82-90; bb.

Hardee, Julia A.; 71-75, 82; e, l, m; Mrs. Dr. Curtis, Kirkville, N. Y.

Hardee, Jennie; 68-72; e, h; Mrs. Chas. Lillie, Pa.; dec.

Harmon, Martha L.; 70-74; i, q; Mrs. Fairchild, N. Y. city, her husband a teacher.

Hasper, Miss; 73; u; Mrs. James Dohney.

Hatfield, Grace A.; 78-92; q, *

Havens, Debora; 90.

Hawley, Giles F.; 73; a; dec.

Hawley, Irene C.; 82-86; Mrs. Nims, Watertown, N. Y.

Hawley, Mary; 74-75; p, s.

Hay, George W.; 75; w. sch.

Hay, Ida M.; 75-79, 82-92; m, q, s, *

Hay, Jennie A.; 75-83; d; Brooklyn, N. Y.

Hayden, Frank A.; 64-66; Mrs. Dan'l Walter, Utica, N. Y.

Hayden, Madaline; 64-65; h, l, married.

Hayden, Anna E.; 63-65, 67, 72, 73, 75-86; d, e, i, Syr.

Hayes, Mary; 72-81; b, Mrs. Nicholas Richmond, Syr.

Hayes, Ella; 71-92; d. *

Haynes, James C.; 76; w. sch.

Hadden, Hattie C.; 90-92; e, *

Henley, Sarah F.; 81. 92; d, *

Hennings, Kate; 66-72; b; dec.

Hicks, Mary D.; 68-79; a; supervisor of Drawing, Prangs, Boston, Mass.

Hickcock, Mary P.; 58-59; b; married, dec.

Hickox, Laura E.; 90-92; t, *

Hitchings, Mary E.; 82-92; x. *

Hill, Miss A.; 54; u.

Hinman, Orren C.; 70-80; p; Los Angelos, Cal.

· Hoagland, Martha; 73; u.

Hodge, Elizabeth A.; 68-92; h, l, *

Hogan, Emma; 84-92; g, *

Hogan, Mary E.

Hogan, Eleanor F.; 82-92; h, *

Holmes, Grace E.; 66, 67, 71-73; d, h; killed in accident at Baptist Church, 73.

Holmes, Theo. A,; 66-78; d, e; Mrs. Sanford.

Holihan, Ella M.; 78-92; u, *

Holmes, Hattie N.; 75 ; e; Mrs. Will Hind, Syr.

Hollister, Kate H.; 67-71; o.

Holkins, Anna E.; 81-92 ; i, j ; Mrs. Blant, Syr.

Hollenbeck, Jessie L.; 88-92; l, *

Hood. Emma F.; 65-70, 75-77; o.

Hooper, J. W.; 64—; u ; *; Camillus.

Hopkins, Charlotte; 52, 53; c; Mrs. Upson, widow, Syr.

Hopkins, Fanny H.: 72-75; l; Mrs. Henry Hooker, Syr.

Horner, Clara I.; 70-80; o, n; Hastings, N. Y.

Hotchkins, Blanche M.; 89-92; s, *

Hotchkins, Mary T.; 68-72; f, *

Hotchkins, Ella M.

Hough. Mrs. O. M.; 54, 55; l.

House, Louisa; 62.

Howe, Carrie E.; 73-86; o, p; Mrs. W. S. Barnum, Syr.

Howe, Grace M.; 90-92; s, *

Howard, Frederick; 86-88 ; a, *; Providence, R. I.

Howlet, Ida; 74-75; f; Mrs. R. Stone, Marcellus, N. Y.

Hoye, Anna L.; 63-73, 75-85; d, q, aa; married, Chicago.

Hoye, Julia E.; 67-74; i, q; married.

Hudson, Miss ——; 68, 69; b.

Hull, Harriet; 50; f.

Hull, Anna L.; 68, 69.

Humphrey, Elizabeth; 53.

Hungerford, Mary; 87-90; b.

Huntington, Laura H.

Hurst. Ella; 65-68; p; dec.

Hunt, Virginia E.; 60; h.

Hurst, Margaret; 57-76, 81-90; k, o, l, m, s.

Hurst, Mary; 67-92; k, l, m, *

Hurd, Bessie L.; 88-92; z, *

Merrick, Libbie F.; 72-76; p; Mrs. Jacoby, Syr.

Metzger, Lizzie; 88-92; s, *

Merriam, Anna C.; 59-60; p.

Miller, Georgiette; 53.

Miller, G. M.; 50-52; w. sch.

Miller, May; 82-86! l, m; Mrs. David Taggart, Syr.

Miller, Geo. A.; 55, 57, 76-81 ; w. sch.

Miller, Mrs. Geo. A.; 55-57, 71-81; h, l, m; dec.

Minton, Nellie; 70, 71; bb.

Mills, Carrie B.; 87-92; n,*

Montague, Louise; 60-66; b, d; Mrs. Robinson, Syr.

Moriarity, Anna C.; 79-92; b, c. *

Morehouse, Maria ; 70, 72-92; d, f; *

Morehouse, Mrs. Wallace; 64; l; dec.

Morgan, Elizabeth F.; 50-54; h, l.

Morgan, Mary.; 62-63.

Moore, Margaret; 53, 59-69, 74-92; h, i, p, *

Moore, Ellen ; 72-92; h, i. *

Morrissey, Agnes B.; 83-92 ; s, m, *

Morris, Carrie L.; 54-63; p,q, s; Mrs. Penning, California.

Morris, Laura ; 57-62 ; o.

Morris, Mary F.; 83-92 ; p, q. *

Monroe, Weed H.; 75-78; w. sch.

Morse, Amelia A.; 90-92; u, *

Moulton, Sophia M.; 68-69.

Morse, May; 83-85; x.

Moulton, Ann; 68; h; died 70.

Moss, Carrie; 83-85; q.

Moss, Louise P.; 55-60; p, q.

Monroe, Julia A.; 91, 92; y, *

Mulhern, Mary; 87-92; b, *

Munger, Mary C.; 60; p.

Munger, Emma H.; 72-76; s; Brooklyn, N. Y.

Munger, Mrs. Clarissa; 74-85; p; Mrs. Barker, Buffalo, N. Y.

Murphy, Kittie; 67-69.

Murphy, Mary S.; 69-92; l, m, *

Murray, Mary; 72-86; d; Mrs. O'Donovan, Syr.

Murray, Sarah I.; 82-92; d, *

Murray, Mary; 80-82; bb.

Murray, Julia R.; 86-92; d, *

Murray, Katherine; 85-92; f, g, *

Murray, Ella A.; 85-92; g, *

Nearing, Miss; 58; w.

Newman, W. W.; 47, 48; p, u, †; So. Onondaga, N. Y.

Newman, Mrs. W. W.; 48; p, †; So. Onondaga, N. Y.

Newman, Rachel ; Mrs. Peck, Cazenovia, N. Y.

Nichols, Catharine A.; 70 ; m ; dec.

Nicholson, Mary E.; 70-85; c, o; Mrs. Wheeler, widow, Syr.

Nicholson, Anna J.; 77-86; c, s; Mrs. Charles Skiff ; Salina.

Noble, Fanny.

Noxon, Margaret; 59; p; Milwaukee, Wis.

Noxon, M. Elizabeth ; 70-71 ; h.

Noxon, Fanny I.; 72-86 ; h; Mrs. Charles Hudson, Syr.

Northrup, Addie ; 71, 72 : w.

Northrup, Mary C.; 86-92; x, *

Ogle, Anna; 65-67 ; d; Mrs. M. V. B. Hart.

Olcutt, Mrs. Mary A. (Morwick); 60-67; k, q; Syr.

Olds, Emma J.; 69-71; c, o; Erie, Pa.

O'Brien, Mary; 89-92; p, *

O'Dwyre, Mary T.; 78-92; m, n, *

O'Donnell, Mary G.; 91-92; f, g, *

O'Keefe, Mary; 70-76; bb.

Otis, Josephine; 62-65; d, l, q, s; Mrs. Henry Rowling, Syr.

Overacker, Minnie E.; 85-92; a, *

Owen, Nancy ; 57-62 ; d, e ; married.

Owen, Margaret; 62; c.

Packard, Mrs. Jennie; 71-76; m, s; Denver, Colo.

Packard, Nellie F.; 77-81; c, s; Mrs. Woodhull, Syr.

Pain, Susan A.; 77-81; o; Mrs. Robert S. Thompson, Montreal.

Palmer, Helen A.; 48-49; f.

Parish, Mrs. Maria (Burk) ; 57-92; d, l, p, q, aa, *

Parker, Mrs. Libbie (Van Wagoner); 64-73, 83-87; b, p, l, s; now Mrs. Abbott, Syr.

Pattison, M. Louise; 68-78, 90-92; a, p, q, *

Perkins, Ella M.; 69, 70; m; dec.

Perry, Mrs. M. J. (Hopkins); 57-82; a, b, p; died, 83.

Perry, Mary A.; 68-70; c.

Pitkin, Carrie I.; 83-86; a; Mrs. McDowell, Elmira, N. Y.

Pierce, Kate J.; 63; d; Brooklyn, N. Y.

Pierce, Mrs. Maria L. (Isham); 52, 53, 67-75; c, o; died, 85, Watertown, N. Y.

Pierson, Miss; 71.

Pharis, Alice E.; 88-92; u, *

Pharis, Mary; 55; u.

Phelps, Abbey L.; 56-57 ; p, m, d; Mrs. Titus Moran, widow, died, 72.

Phelps, Julia E.; 71-75; 78, 79; b, x; married.

Phelps, Mrs.; 75, 76; u; Homer, N.Y.

Phillips, Laura M.; 70-74; c, o; Mrs. Barber, Syr.

Phillips, Rachel C.; 75, 76; l; Canada.

Phillips, Sarah R.; 64-77; l, m; Mrs. Homer Butts, Elbridge.

Plaisted, Flora.

Plumb, Helen A.; 72-74; s; Mrs. G. L. Bonta, dec.

Poole, Katie B.; 57-64, 66-86, 91-92; h, l, nn, *; Mrs. Baldwin, widow

Pomeroy, Harriet; 49; l.

Porter, Jane; 53-55; d, h; Mrs. Geo. Robinson, Milwaukee.

Porter, Dr. W. W.; 52-53; u; dec.

Post, Helen M.; 78-90; e.

Post, Clara H.; 89-92; p, *

Powers, Ida L.; 73, 78-86; b, c; Mrs. Frank Waite, Syr.

Powers, Nora; 87-92; j, *

Pratt, S. Maria; 59-92; c, d, h, *

Pratt, Anna S.; 59-61; d, p.

Pratt, Orpha J.; 65-67; aa; Kansas;

Prescott, Miss K. E.; 44; u.

Prendergast, Mary F.; 78-92; o, p, *

Prudhon, Lydia; 87-89; j.

Pruyn, Rosetta; 51; u; Mrs. Glass, Chattanooga.

Quigley, Julia E.; 77-92; l, m,*

Rae, May L.; 82-92; h, *

Randall, Nellie L.; 83-86 ; s; Mrs. Lighton, Syr.

Rautenburgh, Emma; 82-89; e; Mrs. Autman, Des Moines, Iowa.

Raymond, R. R.; 55-56; a; New York.

Raymond, W. W.; 64-65; h.

Rector, Nellie A.; 81-86; m; Syr.

Redy, Josephine L.; 90-92; t, *

Redhead, Charlotte; 68-76; f; Mrs. Richards, Syr.

Reed, Mrs. Carrie I.; 77-80; p.

Reese, Emma C.; 56-57; p.

Reigel, Eliza M.; 60-71; d, s; Mrs. Dugger, Missouri.

Reigel, Emma L.; 69-72.

Reis, Lydia; 90-92; a, *

Rellis, Nellie; 87-92; j, *

Reynolds, Mrs. Mary C.; 72-79; q, s; W. Superior.

Reynolds, Bertha M.; 70; q; Chicago, Ill.

Reynolds, G. D.; 49; l.

Reynolds, Mrs. G. D.; 41-51.

Reynolds, Helen; 91-92; bb.

Rhoades, Mary P.; 75-78; Brockport Normal school.

Rhoades, Clara; 74-90; l; Mrs. Oscar Austin, Syr.

Rice, Helen P.; 57; f.

Richardson, Miss A. E.; 63-67; h, p; Mrs. Tuttle (Rev.), Canastota, N. Y.

Richardson, Mrs. Josephine S.; 58-61; p.

Richford, Honora; 89-92; b; *

Richardson, W. Lock (Prof.); 72.

Rill, Blossom E.; 91, 92; t, *

Roach, Miss O. C.; 63, 64; f.

Robacher, Mrs. Zillah R. (Clark); 68-69; d.

Robbins, M. Anna; 79-86; l, m, h; Mrs. Willis Malone, Los Angeles, Cal.

Roberts, Laura A.; 44-49; u.

Robinson, Charlotte; 54, 55; l.

Robinson, Miss; 67; w.

Robinson, Harriet L.; 59-66; d.

Roberts, Louisa W.; 81-92; x, y, *

Roblin, Ida A.; 74-75; l; Mrs. Hardendorf, dec.

Rogers, Margaret; 90-92; f, *

Rogers, Ella P.; 78-80; h, c; Syr.

Rogers, Lizzie M.; 74-92; f; *

Rollins, Geo. W.; 77-81; a, *; Boston. Mass.

Rood, Cora; 62-64; c,

Rose, Miss C. R.; 53-55.

Rose, Louisa A.; 62-64; aa; Manlius.

Rose, Anna C.; 53-55; c.

Rosenthal, Belle; 85-92; i, *

Rounds, Fanny; 63-64; d; Mrs. Whitaker, died, Brooklyn,

Roundy, Charles O.; 52-70; a, b, f; died, 92, Skaneateles.

Roundy, Mrs. C. O.; 59-63; h; Skaneateles, N. Y.

Russel, Charles F.; 77; w. sch.

Russel, Mrs. Clara A.; 68, 69; l, m.

Ryan, Nellie; 87-92; w, u, *

Ryan, Esther F.; 82-92; u, *

Ryan, Margaret T.; 83-92; v, *

Ryan, Mary A.; 90-92; t, *

Ryan, Mrs. Louisa A. (Gebhart); 83-92; n, *

Ryan, Nellie J.; 90-92; p, *

Ryan, Kate A.; 91, 92; y, *

Ryan, Emma; 91-92; y, *

Ryan, Joanna C.; 67-, w.

Ryan, Josephine; t.

Sloan, Harriet; 50; Mrs. Hutchinson died; 53.

Slocum, Sarah E.; 54-62; p, l; sister of Gen. Slocum, dec.

Slocum, Kate O.; 66-71; l; Mrs. Butler, Oswego, N. Y.

Slocum, Mercle; 54-63; i, p; Mrs. Boon, Oakland, Cal.

Smith, Edward; 48-65, 80-92; b, c, d, h, *, †.

Smith, Mrs. E.; 50; b; dec.

Smith, Minnie; 60, 61, 83-84; x.

Smith, Eva L.; 68-71; b; Mrs. Eugene B. Squire, died 76.

Smith, Mary A.; 82-92; f, *

Smith, Carrie S.; 70-73; i; Mrs. William Reid, Syr.

Smith, Mrs. M. W. (Terheun) 61-66; b, p.

Smith, Martha E.; 78-81; s; Mrs. Thomas Dalton, Syr.

Smith, Louise; 78-89; o, m; Cor. Univ.

Smith, Kate; 86-89; s, aa; Syr.

Smith, Augusta; 91-92; s, *

Snelle, Louise; 89-92; r, *

Snyder, Margaret; 82-84; o.

Soldan, Rev. Charles; 69-71; a; dec.

Soloman, Rachel; 91-92; x, *

Sprole, Libbie C.; 81-88; o; Mrs. Earnest Smith; dec.

Sprole, Mary; 78-92; d, *

Sprole, Fanny S.; 88-92; e, *

Stafford, Mrs. Margaret; 59-70; o, q., Dakota.

Stafford, Sarah F.; 68-69; q.; Mrs. James Weismore.

Stacy, John; 53; c; died 83.

Stacy, Margaret; 72-79; c; Mrs. Chapman, dec.

Stanley, Mary; 89-90; e, *

Stanton, Mary H.; 74-92; l, *

Stanton, Margaret E.; 57-61; d, h, l, now Dr. Stanton, Syr.

Stanton, Nehemiah; 45-48; f, u; New York City.

Stanton, Mrs. N. P.; 46-48; f; New York City.

Stanton, Cordella; 46; u.

Stanton, Ella C.; 75-84; h, l; Mrs. Henry Phillips, Syr.

Stearns, Allein M.; 69; h.

Steigor, Bertha; 90-92; i, *

Stetson, R. R.; 49-51; h; died, 51.

Stetson, Mrs. Ellen R. R.; 49-51, 57; f, h, *

Steele, James; 73-75; w. sch.

Stevens, S. Elizabeth; 56-60; p.

Stevens, Frances M.; 63-64; p; dec.

Stevens, Elizabeth J.; 56, 57; Mrs. Jed Barber.

Stevens, Mary F.; 62, 68-70; h, p; Mrs. Hasbrook, Syr.

Stevens, Florence M.; 64-66; b, c; Mrs. Young, Green Point.

Stevens, Carrie I.; 75, 81-90; l; married, Cincinnati.

Stevens, Mary E.; 73-74; l.

Stewart, Bessie; 64.

Stilwell, Anna M; 58-63; p; married.

Stilwell, Giles H.; 87; u.

Stone, Mary; 69, 70; p.

Stone, Harriet D.; 68-69; p; Mrs. Watkins, Syr.

Strause, Simon; 61-64; d, o; teacher of German

Strause, Sophia; 72-74; f; Rochester, N. Y.

Strong, Harriet F.; 89-92; l, *

Street, Anna A.; 60-70; c, d.

Sullivan, Minnie C.; 87-92; g.

Sullivan, Lizzie; 81-86; e; dec.

Sullivan, Mary L.; 78-81; f.; dec.

Sullivan, Mary A.; 78-86; d; Mrs.Dr. Fry, Syr.

Summerbill, L. S.; 72-73; p.

Sutton, Sadie; 91, 92; y, *

Swan, Ellen O.; 58-64.

Swain, Clementena; 61-63; k.

Swanger, Maria M.; 68-70; a.

Sweeney, Ellen M.; 77-79; bb.

Sykes, Mary E.; 69-86 ; h, k, l, s ; Syr.

Talbott, Elias; 59; u.

Tallman, Kate E.; 60, 61; p; Mrs. Baker, Syr.

Taylor, G. N.; 49; b.

Taylor, Joseph W.; 73-76; l; in business, Syr.

Taylor, Mrs. J. W.; 74-75; a.

Terry, Frank; 51, 53; s.

Terry, Ida B.; 66-73; e, o.

Terry, Grace E.; 70-74 ; l ; Mrs. Avery, Falmount, Syr.

Terry, Libbie ; 66-81 ; d, p ; Mrs. Gage, Mich.

Terwilliger, Sarah; 65-92; l, n, *; Pr.

Thomas, Mary Jane; 52; h.

Thomas, Mrs. L. E.; 69-92; x, y, *, †; Prin.

Thompson, Mrs. Sarah M.; 72-92 ; g, k, u, w, *

Thompson, Ella B.; 84-89; x, *

Thompson, H. A.; 81; x.

Thurber, Samuel ; 72-78 ; a ; Girls' High school; Boston.

Thurston, Millie M.; 85-89; u.

Tiffany, Ellen; 60, 61; e; Mrs. Brockway.

Titus, Oscar W.; 42 ; u.

Titus, Ellen ; 59; u.

Tomlinson, Nettie A.; 84-92; t.

Town, Agnes M.; 81-92; u, *

Town, Alice S.; 78-92; s, *

Town, Margaret A.; 65-77; f, k, l; Mrs. Hart, Chicago.

Townsend, Maria M.; 65-74; l.

Traugot, Minnie; 89-92; e, *

Tripp, Mary; 54; u.

Tubbert, Agnes; 81-92; b, *

Tucker, Hattie M.; 70, 75, 76 ; o, w; Mrs. Coykendall, Syr.

Tufts, Sarah E.; 66, 67; aa.

Truair, Mary; 66; p, q; Mrs. Dudley, Syr.

Turner, Aurora H.; 50, 53-68; b, c, q; Mrs. Todd, San Diego, Cal.

Turner, Ellen C.; 52-56-63, 65-76; b, c, l; teacher of drawing. Portland, Oregon.

Usenbents, Agnes; 75-79; b; Mrs. Wilson R. Hare, Syr.

Usenbentz, Belle; 79-92; b, *

Underwood, Sarah J.; 74-76, 79-80; l, m, s; Syr.

Van Antwerp, Mary A. (Roney); 70-92 ; m, *; Prin.

Van Brocklyn, William ; 49-50; p; farmer, Pompey, N. Y.

Vandenburg, Jane; 48-56; h.

Vandenburg, Sarah; 55-58; h, p; married and moved west.

Van Frankan, Miss; 78; w; Mrs. Fred Thompson, Auburn, N. Y.

Van Hoesen, Fanny L.; 82–86; l, m; Mrs. Geo. Titsworth, Plainfield, N. Y.

Van Hoesen, Frances L.; 82–86; m, q; Mrs. Arthur Titsworth, Plainfield, N. Y.

Van Keuren, Mary; 85–90; x; married.

Van Tassel, Alice; 64–69; b, d; married; resides in Denver.

Van Tassel, Eliza; 57–67; b, d; dec.

Van Waganen, Rhoda; 66, 68–72; f, h; Mrs. Starin, Syr.

Van Waganen, Miss; 69–70.

Van Wagner, Ellen; 55, 56; h.

Vischer, Mary A.; 65–69; q; married.

Vrooman, Miss N. M.; 44; u.

Wadsworth, Julia S.; 68–71; a.

Wagner, Ella; 55, 56; l.

Wall, Mary E.; 80–92; u, *

Wall, Anna A.; 81; g; Mrs. Charles Burke, Brooklyn, N. Y.

Wall, M. Emma; 74–92; u, *

Wands, Emily E.; 68, 70–75; c; Mrs. Gregory; dec.

Walrod, Virginia E.; 58–59; h.

Walsh, Anna L.; 80–92; h, i, *

Walsh, Ellen; 76–77; bb.

Warne, Adalaide A.; 76–86; e, l; Syr.

Warner, Adeline; 54–56; d, h.

Warner, Dora; 66–69; c; Mrs. George Le Roy, Bradford, Pa.

Waters, Alice E.; 65–73; k, l, m; married; Pennsylvania.

Watson, Bruce M.; 86–92; a, l, * prin.

Weaver, Jennie; 58, a.

Weaver, Martha; 52–54; h.

Weigel, Libbie; 78–92; d, *

Weiskotten, Amelia; 76–92; a, e, l, †

Weiskotten, Louisa M.; 79–92; d, c,*

Weiskotten, F. W. (Rev.); 62–63; d; Philadelphia, Pa.

Welch, Emma A.; 75–90; o, p, l; died in 90 in her work.

Weld, Sarah S.; 58, 59; p.

Wells, Charles R.; 79–92; * †; writing; Syr.

Wells, Mary E.; 69, 70; o.

Wells, Laura A.; 64, 65; d; Mrs. Chapman; dec.

Wescott, Carrie E.; 69–72; s.

Wescott, Julia E.; 65–69, 72–74; s; Mrs. Cleveland.

Wescott, Mary A.; 65–68; l.

Wescott, Minnie E.; 82–92; A; x, *

Whalen, Abbey; 83–92; s, *

Wheaton, Myron; 51–58; s; member of assembly, Northfield, Minn.

Whelock, Anna A; 57–65; 67–71; b, p, l; Mrs. Henry A. Maynard, Onondaga Valley.

Wheeler, E. M.; 66–71; b; killed by an accident, 92.

Wheeler, Nettie; 68–70; f, h; dec.

Wheelock, Elijah O.; 42; u.

White, R. Bruce; 69, 75–76, 77–88, 90–92; b, p, l, s; †; in business, Syr.

White, Charles E.; 87–92; e, * †; Pr.

White, Henrietta B.; 40–45, 46–53, 73–74; d, f, u; Mrs. Hewes, 50; Hoopstown, Ill.

White, Louisa; 51–53; d; married, west.

White, Sarah L.; 52–54; h, p.

White, Jennie E.; 78–92; t, w, * †

White, Mrs. Jennie; 69–71, 85; x; Mrs. Dowd.

BIOGRAPHICAL SKETCHES

ALBERT GLEASON SALISBURY

was born in August, 1813, at Seneca Castle, Ontario
county, N. Y. He was educated at Whitesboro and
Pompey academies. His first teaching probably was at
a small district school in the town of Fabius. Afterwards, probably 1838–9, he opened a select school in the
session room of the First Presbyterian church, then
located on ground now occupied by McCarthy's dry
goods store. For two weeks he remained in the faithful discharge of duties with only one pupil. After that
discouraging beginning his prospects brightened and
other pupils filled the room. He also taught in Lodi
in a small building on East Genesee street, on the ground
where the late Wadsworth Clark's house now stands.
While he was engaged as teacher in this vicinity,
a new building, containing one room, was being erected
on the ground where the old Putnam building now
stands. There were two entrances with a small ante-
room between. This was considered an ornament to the
small village. Mr. Salisbury whose reputation had been
made by his successes in the preceding schools, was solicited to become the principal and with two assistants,

Miss Mary Bradley and Miss Sarah Tallman, who afterward became Mrs. Salisbury, he opened the school in
the autumn of 1840.   Miss Tallman was obliged to hear
classes in the little ante-room before mentioned.   Mr.
Salisbury and Miss Tallman were married in October,
1842, and both continued teaching.

Mr. Salisbury remained in this school till about 1842
or '43 when a successful effort was made for the enlargement of No. 7.   While this was in progress he taught a
select school over where Grant & Dunn's hardware
store is now located, and afterward in the session room
of the Old Congregational church.   When the enlarged
No. 7 was finished, Mr. Salisbury again became its
principal where he remained until the three villages,
Salina, Syracuse and Lodi, were chartered as the City
of Syracuse.

At the organization of the Board of Education, Mr.
Salisbury was elected the first clerk and secured for the
new school system a good beginning.   This work did
not seem congenial to him and he resigned his position
in February, 1850, to resume the principalship of No. 7.
In June, 1850, He was re-elected clerk and continued
in that position till May, 1851, when he again resigned
and was again appointed principal of No. 7.   He remained in this position till 1854, when he left and
opened a private school in the Myers Block which was
furnished with the best appliances known at that time,
and his school became very popular.   He continued in

this enterprise till September, 1857, when he became principal of No. 7 and remained till he was appointed paymaster in the army, 1864. He continued in that office till 1867. He was soon after appointed warden of the Auburn prison, where he remained something over a year. At the resignation of Mr. Roundy from the principalship of the Syracuse High school in the spring of 1871, Mr. Salisbury, at the earnest solicitation of the Board of Education, consented to fill the position till the close of that school year, which he did to the entire satisfaction of all interested. This ended his work as an educator. He died in 1874.

E. A. SHELDON, A.M., Ph.D.

was born at Perry Centre, N. Y., in 1823, and received his early education from home training on the farm and among the scenes of country and farm life, attending the common schools of that day. At the age of seventeen he attended a private school where the first impulse for real and progressive advancement was received. He entered Hamilton College at twenty-one years of age but was obliged to leave at the close of the junior year because of failing health. He went to Oswego and started in business which was not successful, but while thus engaged, the condition of the poor and ignorant caused him, with others, to form an Association, for providing a home for orphans and a free school for the children of the poor.   Mr. Sheldon was induced to become its teacher in the winter of 1848–49.   This was the beginning of the free graded schools and of the Oswego Orphan Asylum of Oswego.

In 1849, he married Miss Frances A. B. Stiles who has been his constant supporter through all his life work.   In 1850 a private school was started by him in the old United States Hotel and while engaged in this he applied for the position of superintendent of public schools of Syracuse.   During the two years he remained in this work he was instrumental in consolidating the district school libraries into the present Central Library; published the first annual report of the Board of Education; and was largely instrumental in establishing the High school of this city.

He returned to Oswego in 1853 to take charge of the schools of that city as clerk of the Board of Education, and while organizing them he established arithmetic schools for boys and young men employed on the lakes in summer, and in 1859 established an unclassified school for those unable to attend regularly throughout the year.

He visited Toronto where he saw the collections of appliances used abroad, especially in the London Home and Training school.   Many of these were secured and a detailed plan for their use and introduction into the course of study was devised.

He presented his plan to the Board of Education and

asked for trained teachers to carry on the work of object teaching put before them.

They consented on condition that it should be without cost to the city. To meet the expense the interested teachers gave one-half of their salaries for one year to this object. Not only the people of Oswego, but many outside were opposed to the project, but Mr. Sheldon was finally vindicated by resolutions passed by a committee of which Prof. Green of Brown University, was chairman in 1865.

Mr. Sheldon organized a Training school for educating teachers in 1863, which was afterward adopted by the State as the Oswego Normal and Training school.

In 1869 he resigned the superintendency of the city schools and devoted all his energies to the Normal school. Again home opposition was stirred up against him in 1872, which with his other arduous labors undermined his health and he offered his resignation, which was not accepted but he was relieved from his duties and his salary continued. He was able to return to his work in 1881. In this year the Kindergarten was added to the course of study.

It is now nearly forty years since Mr. Sheldon left Syracuse schools and yet he is still enthusiastic and progressive, with no abatement of faith or of hope for the future in progressive educational methods.

GEORGE L. FARNHAM

was born in Richfield, Otsego county, N. Y., in 1824 ; educated in the common schools till 1840 when he removed to Watertown and attended the Black River academy. After teaching part of the year (1846) he went to the Albany State Normal school, then under the charge of David P. Page and graduated in 1847. He came to Syracuse in 1852, taking charge of Jefferson school (No. 3). In 1855 he was chosen superintendent of the city schools and continued eight years in that work. After a short time he was called to superintend the Binghamton schools and remained five years where he remodeled the whole system, inluding buildings, course of study, and methods of teaching : introducing what has since been called the "Sentence Method" and which has been acknowledged by many as the philosophical method. From there he went to Council Bluffs, Ia., and remained three years and then to Peru, Neb., to take charge of the State Normal school where he has been nine years.

Mr. Farnham has been a student of psychology, philosophy and professional teaching. He regards his work in this city as the inspiration and the beginning of his educational career, which has been remarkably successful.

CHARLES EDWARD STEVENS

was born in the city of Buffalo, on the 20th day of

May, 1836. His father, Augustus C. Stevens, was of New England ancestry, and a prominent business man: who died at the age of 37 years. His mother, Elizabeth Breese, came from English and Dutch stock ; his maternal grandfather was an officer in the Revolution, and a near relative of Professor Samuel Finley Breese Morse. Charles Edward is the youngest son and his early years were spent at his grandfather's homestead at Sconondoa, near Oneida, N. Y. He attended school at Cazenovia seminary, and afterwards at Fulton, N.Y., and entered upon the study of law in the office of Governor William M. Fenton of Flint, Mich. Shortly after being admitted to the bar of that State he removed to Syracuse in 1857, and for a short time was in the office of Gen. William J. Hough. He was admitted to practice law in the New York Courts, and was for many years a partner of Hon. N. F. Graves of this city. Mr. Stevens in politics has always been a Democrat of the most steadfast faith.

In 1863, at the time when party spirit ruled high, due largely to the war issues prevailing at that time, the Board of Education of the city of Syracuse passed under the control of the democratic party—they having elected the majority of the school commissioners; it was thought and claimed by them that they were in duty bound to place the public schools under the charge and direction of a superintendent who was a Democrat in politics. Several gentlemen now prominent in the

affairs of the city, were candidates for the position, and
the strife for the office became so warm and spirited
that after balloting many times, and adjourning from
day to day, it became apparent that a compromise can-
didate must be brought into the field ; and at the urg-
ent solicitation of the leaders of the party, Mr. Stevens,
reluctantly consented to the use of his name, and he
was elected superintendent of the public schools on the
258th ballot.   Mr. Stevens came to the office with no
experience as a teacher, and with but limited knowledge
of the educational work required in the public schools,
but he had a good fund of common sense and rare tact in
acquiring the business management of school affairs.
He had the good sense not to presume to lead in educational work, except so far as he oppropriated the suggestions and advice of the best teachers in the employ
of the Board.

On his election he was thoroughly conservative, and
opposed to all changes in the corps of teachers then in
the schools, believing that tried and experienced talent,
notwithstanding the question of politics, would serve
the schools with greater fidelity and do better work than
others of less experience and unacquainted with this
particular field.   To a large extent he succeeded in his
efforts and persuaded the Board to retain largely the
old corps of teachers.

In his efforts for the schools he was ably seconded by
members of the Board of Education, then composed of

the Rev. Samuel J. May, N. B. Smith and others, and also by such tried teachers as the late Prof. Charles O. Roundy, Ansel E. **Kinne, A.** G. Salisbury, Superintendent Smith, Sarah M. Arnold, **Sylvia J. Eastman,** Martha S. Clapp and in fact by the whole body of teachers then in the employ of the Board. During the three years he was superintendent of the public schools they suffered no detriment in his hands, but made good progress under his management and direction.

In 1866, when Mr. Stevens retired from office, he received from the teachers a beautiful token of their regard for him, and he had the honor of naming his successor in office, Mr. Edward Smith, who was elected to the position at his advice and solicitation.

Mr. Stevens is now connected with the law firm of Stevens & Butterfield, of this city, and doing a fair business, leading a quiet and unostentatious life, his only ambition being to fill the measure of good citizenship in this community.

DR. JOHN H. FRENCH

was born in Batavia, July 7, 1824. His father was killed when he was quite young. Most of his education was obtained from the common schools, by attending during the winter and working in summer.

The first ten cents he ever earned was spent for a Webster's spelling book. At sixteen he spent a winter in the Cary Collegiate institute. He spent one or two terms in the Clarence academy, Erie county, and taught his first school when he was seventeen years old. He afterward taught in Pembroke, Stafford, and Seneca Castle. At this last place, at the age of twenty-one he began his work as a mathematician and an author by revising Adams' arithmetic. He taught one year in Geneva Lyceum, one year in Phelps Union school. From there he went to Keene, N. H., and completed his revision above mentioned under the supervision of Mr. Adams. He wrote Adams's mental arithmetic, mensuration, book-keeping. These were entirely his, but formed a part of the Adams series.

He was principal of the High school, Clyde, N. Y., three years, and three years principal of the academy at Newtown, Ct. He published twelve town and city maps from actual surveys in the central part of this State and in connection with Robert P. Smith of Philadelphia, the map of the State of New York accompanied with a Gazetteer, the two being sold for $10. All the work except printing and engraving, being done under his supervision.

He revised Robinsons's mathematical series and wrote the greater part of the Algebra. His demonstration of the binomial theorem was for a long time known as "French's."

He lived in Syracuse from 1855 to 1867 giving his time to institute work and the preparation of a series

of arithmetics which bore his name. He was made
superintendent of the city schools in 1865, but resigned
after a few months to become principal of the experi-
mental department of the State Normal school at
Albany. In 1870 he was elected secretary of the Board
of Education of Vermont where he remained five years.
In 1878 he became principal of the State Normal school
at Indiana, Pa., and remained three years. Overwork
here brought on typhoid fever from which he never re-
gained his accustomed strength and vigor. He took up
the work of institute conductor again and continued it
till his death.

At the age of twenty-three, he married Mary E.
Washburn who survives him. He had two daughters
both of whom died, one in Syracuse, 1862, and the
other in Boston, in 1888, aged 25. This was a severe
affliction.

His last work was the preparation of a paper on drawing to be read at the meeting of school commissioners
held in New York, January 8, 1889, but he was obliged
to send it on to be read. He died December 23, 1888,
leaving his life-long companion alone.

This is but a brief statement of the work accomplished by Dr. French. His life is an inspiration
to all young men who may come in contact with his
work.

[NOTE.—This history would be incomplete without the following brief notice of the author, Mr. Smith, and his connection with the public schools of Syracuse. I take pleasure in presenting it.   A. B. BLODGETT.]

EDWARD SMITH,

the writer of this history, was born December 30, 1817, in Skaneateles, N. Y., where he lived till he was ten years old, when his father moved to Cattaraugus county, and settled on a farm. Mr. Smith attended the public school in the winter and worked on the farm during the summer months till he was nineteen years old. He attended a private school and the academy at Prattsburg, Steuben county, one year each. He commenced what has proved his life work in 1837, teaching in the country districts in the winter, and in a private school in Kentucky one summer term of twenty weeks. He also served as town superintendent in Cattaraugus county for two years, 1839–1840.

Mr. Smith first came to Syracuse in the spring of 1845. He was immediately engaged here, where he has since labored continuously: twenty-five years as a teacher and principal, and twenty-three years as superintendent of the city schools; a total of forty-eight years, out of which period he has not lost one entire year. A simple record of Mr. Smith's personal work in connection with the growth and prosperity, the ups and downs of the school system, would in itself make a complete, an attractive, and a most interesting history.

The public schools of this city, in themselves the essential product of Mr. Smith's life-long labors, present the most worthy testimony of what he has accomplished. He labored early and late, and with fidelity and great earnestness. He conscientiously endeavored to bring teachers and pupils into contact with all that was best and foremost in educational lines; and ever had in mind the elevation of the thought, the intelligence, and the character of the city through the great factor, the public schools. In truth, as we recall that Mr. Smith has for nearly half a century had very much to do in the direction of the work, we are amazed at his ability in keeping abreast of the times; and it is an established fact—even historical — that the Syracuse public schools have been leaders, never laggards, in educational lines.

His annual election for twenty-three consecutive years to the superintendency was the fullest expression of the confidence of successive Boards of Education. Mr. Smith possesses an iron constitution; which in connection with a kindly disposition, clean motives, and earnest purposes, has brought him through his long term of service, a well preserved, active, vigorous man, still busily engaged in the calling which has claimed his whole being, and which he has pursued with tireless energy. The work of such a life is rarely given its full value, and this brief tribute of words but faintly measures its achievements.

SILAS M. BETTS

was born in Borodino on the east shore of Skaneateles lake in 1828. His parents moved soon after to Canton, now called Memphis, where he attended the public schools. He also attended school at Van Buren Centre, now Warners, and afterward, the Onondaga academy and the academy at Homer, while the late Samuel Woolworth was principal. Mr. Betts' first teaching was at Belle Isle, "boarding around," in the winter of 1844–45. He then attended the Normal school at Albany and graduated in 1849. Soon after, he became principal of No. 9, then a small wooden building on West street, Syracuse.

In 1851, Mr. Betts was made principal of No. 11, where he remained till he was appointed principal of No. 7, in 1855. He accepted an appointment as principal of a High school at Niles, Mich., in 1859, and was instrumental in making the schools of the State free to all children. He held teachers' institutes in his own and neighboring counties during vacations, till overwork obliged him to resign. After one year of rest he became vice-principal of the New Jersey State Normal school in 1861, assisting in institute work and continued three years, then resigned.

He now resides on a State farm near Philadelphia, Pa. He aided in organizing the American Guernsey Cattle Club of which he has been the president three years. He says:

"I have lived to see the schools of New York, Michigan and New Jersey made free and vastly improved and have taken a humble part in the work, but my most pleasant memories are connected with the schools of Syracuse."

CHARLES O. ROUNDY

was born in Spafford, Onondaga county, N. Y., May 23, 1823. He received his education in the public schools of his native town and in the Homer, N. Y., academy.

The degree of A.M. was conferred upon him by Hamilton college in 1853. Almost his entire active life has been spent in teaching, beginning in his own town, at eighteen years of age, soon after leaving the academy in Homer. He afterward taught in Skaneateles and Baldwinsville, coming from there to Syracuse at the death of Principal Stetson, to take the place vacated in 1852, where he remained till the establishment of the Syracuse High school in 1855, when he became its first principal. He remained in charge of this school till the spring of 1871, when failing health compelled him to retire.

After a year or two devoted to traveling combined with some light work he again began teaching in the Union Free school at Moravia, N. Y., where he remained ten years. Leaving there, he spent one year and a half in Dakota and then retired to his farm in Skaneateles, N. Y.; but his love for the work prompted him to seek the privilege of teaching in his own district at a nominal salary.

Mr. Roundy has always been noted for his zeal and enthusiasm as a teacher in the small as well as in the larger school, in the primary as well as in the high school. When engaged in teaching no amount of labor was too exacting, that he might have something new to present to his class on the coming day to illustrate the principles to be elucidated or to awaken interest in his pupils. Till late at night with his lamp on the floor and his books around him within easy reach, he would lie at full length, studying and investigating till he had mastered his subject, then with increased enthusiasm appear before his class next day to inspire them with something of his own spirit. His pupils in this city, graduates of the High school for sixteen years, will never forget the love for study and the ambition awakened in them for learning, by his energetic spirit.

Mr. Roundy's work is completed. He died (September 30, 1892) at his home in Skaneateles, leaving a wife and two married daughters. His funeral was attended at Moravia, October 4, where his last important teaching was done, and where many of his pupils were able to show their respect for the memory of a loved and revered teacher.

WILLIAM WILSON NEWMAN

was born at South Onondaga, N. Y., October 5, 1821 ; educated in public and private schools, Onondaga academy, Cazenovia seminary and Albany academy; was admitted to Hamilton college and received an honorary degree of A. M. from Union college. He began teaching at seventeen at Howlett Hill, and taught at Amboy, Geddes, Baldwinsville, Onondaga academy, South Onondaga, Putnam school, in Syracuse, and No. 13, in Buffalo. He was two terms (six years) school commissioner of the second district of Onondaga county, and is now, 1892, Superintendent of the Onondaga Reservation Indian school. He is now living in his 72d year on the farm where he was born.

His wife, Elizabeth Esther Williams, was born at South Onondaga ; educated at Manlius and Chittenango academies ; taught at Manlius, Syracuse and Buffalo, and is now living on the farm with her husband. They were married at the teachers' institute in their schoolhouse, No. 7, the Putnam, and went immediately to their new school, No. 13, in Buffalo, where they taught thirteen years, till sickness caused Mr. Newman to resign his principalship and retire to the home farm.

Both have taught successfully many thousand pupils during over thirty years of teaching life.

ANSEL E. KINNE

was born May 17, 1820, and was the last of eleven children. Ansel received all the education the common district schools provided at that time. At the age of nineteen he attended the academy at Fayetteville, and became inspired with a desire to become a teacher.

His first school met in a log house in the town of DeWitt, and was satisfactory and successful. The next winter he taught in DeWitt, and the following summer entered the seminary at Cazenovia. In the autumn he again entered the seminary, and later was employed to teach the village school. In the spring he returned to Cazenovia, and remained till fitted for college at twenty-four years of age. Failing health made this impracticable.

In the winter of 1845–46, he taught the village school in Fayetteville, and the following winter the DeWitt school, the summer of 1847, the Jamesville school, and the winter of 1848–49, in his own district in DeWitt.

He married Miss Emma Merrick, of this city. In the spring of 1850 he was elected town superintendent of schools of DeWitt.

In the spring of 1851, he removed to Syracuse, built a house in the Fifth Ward, and entered business for four years. In 1855, he was made principal of Prescott school, where he continued till January, 1864, when he received an appointment under General Saxton as Superintendent of Freedmen, at Fernandina, Florida. He remained there three years and was offered the appointment of Superintendent of schools of the State of Florida. This last offer came after he had planned to return north for the education of his children.

After his return, Mr. Camp, the principal of Putnam school, resigned, and Mr. Kinne received the appointment to the position, and remained there till the occupation of the new High school building, when the eighth year pupils from the ward schools were transferred to that building, and the Central Senior school organized with Mr. Kinne as its principal. He remained in this school till June, 1872, when that school was discontinued and Mr. Kinne accepted the principalship of Madison school, which had just been completed. He remained in this school, doing, as he always had, a missionary work in trying to reclaim the truant and disobedient belonging to his school, until his death, January 16, 1890.

EBENEZER BUTLER

was born at Pompey, Onondaga county, N. Y., in May, 1829 ; was educated at Pompey academy, and began the work of a teacher on the last day of the year 1849, in the village of Buch Bond, Wayne county, Pa. In the fall of 1850, he was called to the school in the village of Pleasant Mount, same county and State. He continued at the head of that school till the fall of 1852, when he returned to his native town ; and (excepting three terms), from that date till the year 1863, he was in charge of the public school in the village of Pompey.

In the fall of 1863, he became connected with the public school of Manlius Village, as principal. At the end of a year, and in the fall of 1864, he accepted the position as teacher of the school in the village of Geddes and remained at the head of that school till May, 1866, when he received from the Board of Education, Syracuse, N. Y., the appointment of principal of Seymour school.

He held that position over seven years, and till the fall of 1873 ; when, declining re-appointment, he accepted the position of superintendent of the schools of Whitehall, N. Y.

Serving in that capacity for nine years, and till the fall of 1882, he returned to Onondaga county, and accepted the appointment of principal of Danforth school. He remained in that position five years, till 1887. Declining a re-appointment for 1888, tendered to him by the Board, Professor Butler, after a period of thirty-eight years of continuous and successful service in the work of an educator, retired from active school work, and entered upon the duties of a business career, in the city of Syracuse, in which work he is now engaged.

WALTER A. BROWNELL

was born at Evans Mills, N. Y., March 23, 1838. He graduated from Gouverneur seminary, N. Y., as valedictorian of his class, in 1861; and also from Genesee college, Lima, N. Y., in 1865. He taught in various district schools during his undergraduate work. He was for one term professor of Latin in Falley seminary, at Fulton, N. Y. From 1865 to 1868 he was principal of Red Creek seminary; from 1868 to 1871, principal of Fairfield seminary, N. Y.; from 1871 to 1872, principal of Syracuse High school; and he has been from 1872 to the present time, professor of chemistry and geology in the Syracuse high school.

During the summer vacations from 1881 to 1886, he was professor of geology and mineralogy in the school for teachers at Martha's Vineyard, Mass. He received the title of Ph.D. from Hamilton college, in 1876.

SAMUEL THURBER

was born in Providence, R. I., April 4, 1837. His early education was in the public schools of Providence. He entered Brown university in 1853, but resided there five years, and graduated at 21 in 1858.

His life has been devoted to teaching, excepting a year in the army—1862-1863—and three years during which he traveled on the Pacific coast, principally in Idaho, in the employment of a mining company.

He was principal of the high schools of Hyde Park, Mass., Syracuse, where he remained six years, and Worcester, Mass. His first teaching was in the Providence high school, and he left the post of principal of the classical department of that school in 1865, to enter on the mining venture referred to above.

In 1880, he went to Boston to take a position in the Girls' high school, where he now is filling the post of master in that school, and teaching English.

He says: "I look back on my six years in Syracuse as the pleasantest part of my life."

GEORGE A. BACON

was born at Webster, Mass., January 17, 1847. Prepared for college at Nichols academy, Dudley, Mass. Graduated at Brown university, Providence, R. I., in 1867. Taught one year in Derby, Vt., as principal of Derby academy, and one year as principal of the high school in Gardner, Mass. Spent two years (nearly) in post-graduate study here and in Europe. Taught history and mathematics for three years (1871–1874) in the Brooklyn Polytechnic Institute. Was assistant three years (1874–1877), and principal ten years (1878–1888) in the Syracuse high school. Editor and publisher of *The Academy*, 1886–1892. He received the degree of A.B. from Brown university in 1867, and that of Ph.D., from Hamilton college in 1879.

He resigned his position in the High school, to form a partnership in the publishing house of Allyn & Bacon, where he is now engaged.

R. BRUCE WHITE

was born at Willow Glen, in the town of Skaneateles, November 10, 1839. He received his education in the village school at Mottville, at old district school No. 13, in the town of Skaneateles, and at Monroe Collegiate institute, in Elbridge, N. Y.

In Nov., 1858, he began teaching in District No. 13, Skaneateles, and continued during two winter terms. In 1860, he assumed charge of the Mottville village school, remaining there six years. In April, 1866, he went to Marcellus, and was principal of the union school there for three years.

In the spring of 1869, Mr. White came to Syracuse as principal of Putnam school, resigning in the spring of 1870.

In January, 1874, he was appointed principal of Salina school, remaining there until June, 1877, when he was transferred to Seymour school, continuing in charge until October, 1887.

In January, 1890, he was appointed principal of Madison school, resigning August 1, 1892. For thirty-four years, Mr. White has been a teacher in Onondaga county, and for nearly twenty-four years in the schools of Syracuse.

H. ELBERT BARRETT

was born in 1851.   His early education was commenced in a district school at Hannibal, Oswego county, N. Y. At sixteen, he was placed in Falley seminary, Fulton, then under the charge of an excellent instructor, Prof. J. P. Griffin, where his training continued three years.

After teaching one term in a country district school, he determined to make teaching a vocation, and at once entered the State Normal school at Oswego, in 1872, and graduated from the classical department of that institution.   In the fall of the same year he took charge of the Yates Union school at Chittenango, N. Y., where he remained one year.

In 1873, he was elected to the position of teacher of methods in the State Normal school at Bloomsburg, Pa.   This position was resigned in 1877, when he returned to New York to engage temporarily in newspaper work.

During March, 1881, Mr. Barrett became connected with the public schools of this city as principal of Salina school, which position he still retains.

BRUCE M. WATSON

was born at Windsor, N. Y.. February 28, 1860.   He received his education in the common schools of his native place, and in the public schools of Binghamton,

N. Y. He entered the State Normal school at Oswego, and graduated. He then entered a public school in the suburbs of Binghamton, which has since been annexed to that city, where he continued two years. From there he went to Huguenot, N. Y., and remained one year ; then to Pulaski, N. Y., one year. From the latter place he was offered a position in the Syracuse High school, as teacher of methods in the Teachers' class, and remained till the spring of 1888, when he was appointed temporary principal of Seymour school in place of R. B. White, who was out of school on leave of absence. Mr. White did not return to the position, and Mr. Watson was appointed permanently, which position he has faithfully and acceptably filled to the present time.

A. B. BLODGETT

was born in Mottville, Onondaga county, N. Y., in 1850. He was educated at DeRuyter institute and at Cazenovia seminary. He began teaching in 1870 at Skaneateles Falls, N. Y., and afterward taught in Madison and Onondaga counties. In April, 1873, he took charge of the union school in Tully village, where he remained two years.

From Tully he went to Cazenovia, and entered the seminary as student doing outside tutoring. In 1876–1877, he had charge of the commercial department in

Cazenovia seminary, at the same time continuing his studies.

In the winter of 1875–1876, he left Cazenovia to take charge of the winter school in the First Ward of this city, returning to his studies in April, 1876.

He was elected full instructor in the seminary, in June, 1877, but resigned upon being notified of his election to the principalship of Salina school in this city.

He remained in Salina school till March, 1881, when he was transferred to Prescott school, in the Fourth Ward. He held this position till March 5, 1889, when he was elected superintendent of the schools of Syracuse, N. Y., which position he still occupies.

In October, 1890, at a meeting of the Council of City Superintendents of the State, Mr. Blodgett was chosen chairman of a committee of five to lay before the other educational bodies of the State the advisability of organizing a State Educational Congress to consider the future educational interests of the State. A report was made, and the committee still has the matter in charge.

Mr. Blodgett was president of the New York State Teachers' Association for the year 1892.

CHARLES E. WHITE

was born in the town of Wayne, Trumbull county,

Ohio, August 2, 1848. His parents removed to Cazenovia, N. Y., four years after.

He attended district school till the age of fourteen, and then spent one year in a preparatory school, conducted by Prof. Robert Ellis at Cazenovia, after which he was a student in Cazenovia seminary until the winter of 1867, when he taught his first school at Rebel's Corners near Canastota. The next winter he taught the school at "Old No. 9" near Cazenovia, "boarding round" both seasons, and returning to Cazenovia seminary, after the close of school, each term.

In September, 1869, he was called to the principalship of the Camillus school, remaining four years. His next school was at South Butler, Wayne county, where he taught one year, resigning to take charge of the school at Hannibal, Oswego county, which he resigned after a year, to again take the principalship of the Camillus school, which he held four years longer, resigning on account of ill-health, and for a few months engaging in the manufacture of chairs at Elbridge, N. Y. A vacancy occurring at Cicero he was called to take charge of that school, where he remained till the fall of 1880. He was then elected school commissioner of the third district of Onondaga county, but resigned the office after serving two years, to take the position of superintendent of schools in the village of Geddes.

He served as superintendent three years, and was re-appointed. In March, 1886, Geddes village was annexed to Syracuse, and by a clause in the bill of annexation the superintendent of the schools of Geddes, was placed under the direction of the Board of Education of the city of Syracuse, and Mr. White was appointed principal of Franklin school, where he has remained till the present time. In 1886 Mr. White was chosen president of the New York State Association of School Commissioners and Superintendents, and was president of the Onondaga Educational Council for the year 1888. He is the author of a primary arithmetic entitled Two Years with Numbers, which is used in the public schools of Syracuse and in some other cities.

MRS. L. E. THOMAS

was born in Baldwinsville, Onondaga county; educated at Baldwinsville Academy, and began teaching in 1868 in the town of Van Buren. She came to the village of Brighton in 1869 where she remained till that district became a part of Syracuse. When the new Brighton school was built in 1881 Mrs. Thomas was transferred to the principalship of the Danforth school. She has practically been where she now is from 1869 to 1893.

GEORGE A. LEWIS

was born in the town of Clay, Onondaga county, N. Y., January 29, 1850. ' His early education was received in the district school, and at the age of 17 he commenced teaching.

In the spring of 1869 his family moved to Syracuse and he entered the high school the first session the present building was occupied. After spending one year in this school he taught during the winter terms of 1870 and 1871, and in the spring attended Cazenovia seminary a short term and became the principal of the graded school at North Syracuse, where he remained a year and a half, when he resigned to attend the Oswego Normal school, from which he graduated in the classical course, July, 1877.

Later in the season he was appointed to the principalship of the school at Morristown, N. Y., where a new building had just been erected. After four years of service there in reorganizing the school on the line of advanced educational work which proved eminently successful, impaired health prompted him to resign.

In the fall of 1881 he was elected school commissioner of the first commissioner district of St. Lawrence county. In the fall of 1888 he was appointed assistant in the Syracuse High school, where his untiring energy and the faithful discharge of his duties have made him an important factor in its faculty.

EZEKIEL WILSON MUNDY

was born in Metuchen, Middlesex county, N. J., in 1833. He was graduated from Rochester university in

1860 with the degree of A.B. and took the degree of A.M. in regular course.

He studied theology in the Rochester Theological seminary from which he was graduated in 1863. From the seminary Mr. Mundy went at once to take charge of the First Baptist church, Syracuse, N. Y. He was pastor there for three years, at the close of which he took charge of the Independent church of Syracuse. After a pastorate of thirteen years he resigned in 1879, and took orders in the Protestant Episcopal church.

In 1880, Mr. Mundy was put in charge of the Central Library, which place he still holds.

FREDERICK A. LYMAN

was born in Columbia, Ct., in 1864, and attended a country district school. A love for music became manifest at eleven years of age when he began its study from a primer of music without a teacher and he learned to play on the melodeon.

At fourteen years he began to study the piano and vocal art under teachers in Hartford, Ct. He moved to Rhode Island and at the age of eighteen, after attending a graded school one year, commenced teaching and continued in this work four years, keeping up his musical studies, giving special attention to public school music, theory of music and vocal art. He attended the Normal Music school at Lexington, Mass., in 1886, and taught in the same school four years.

For the past two summers he has taught in the musical department of the American Institute of Normal Methods. He passed a successful examination before the board of the American College of Musicians in 1886, and in 1891 was elected one of the examining board of that organization.

He has done a large amount of musical work outside of the public schools by directing church choirs, instrumental and vocal organizations, by playing church organs and several string and brass instruments. He has written a variety of music, including songs, church music, compositions for military bands and orchestras.

He is the vice-president of the Rhode Island Music Teachers' Association, and of the New York State Association.

Mr. Lyman became the director of music in the public schools of Syracuse, in the autumn of 1888, where he has done most excellent work in developing a taste for the science among teachers and pupils, and is systematizing a complete and thorough elementary course in music.

WILLIAM H. SCOTT

was born September 4, 1844, at Pontiac, Mich.; attended school and prepared for college there, intending to enter Michigan university in September, 1862. But instead, July, 1862, he enlisted in the Mich. Vol. Inf., and remained with his regiment, acting as commissary, till mustered out in July, 1863.

In September, he entered Oberlin college, Oberlin, Ohio, with the class of 1870.   Ill-health compelled him to leave before graduating, but subsequently the degree of A. M. was conferred.

He taught in Michigan, while a student in college. Then in Cleveland, Ohio, under Superintendent A. J. Rickoff, and was principal of the high school at Brooklyn Village, Ohio, one year.

Ill-health induced him to go into business for six years. He then engaged in teaching in the public schools of Omaha, Nebraska, where he remained four years. From there he went to the Michigan Military academy at Orchard Lake, Michigan, for one year as professor of English.   The following year he was principal of the Pontiac High school.

He then engaged in business in Wyoming, Colorado, and Nebraska, finally going to California, and engaged in teaching; giving his time out of school to fruit raising.   He remained in California three years and came to Syracuse in May, 1887, and the following June was elected principal of Porter school.

MARY WINIFRED FLANAGAN

was born at Camillus, Onondaga county, N. Y., Sept., 1861. After completing the regular course of study at the village union school, she commenced teaching at Fairmount, N. Y., in 1880.

Her ambition to be qualified for the best localities prompted her to enter the Oswego Normal school, where she graduated July 6th, 1886. The American Institute of Normal Methods at Nyack-on-the-Hudson, July, 1892, gave her a diploma in music. She also completed the regular three years' course at the H. E. Holt Normal Musical school and Institute of Vocal Harmony at Lexington, Mass., and graduated August, 1892.

In September, 1886, Miss Flanagan was selected principal of " Rock school," in the town of Geddes. Soon after, this part of Geddes became the Ninth Ward of Syracuse, and she with her junior pupils was transferred in Feb., 1887 to May school, where she remained, nearly three years.

In September, 1889, she and her pupils were again transferred to White's hall, and there remained during the construction of the new Delaware school, and the following February was appointed principal of Delaware school, a position which she still holds.

GRADUATES OF THE SYRACUSE HIGH SCHOOL

1856

Rossiter W. Raymond,   Osgood V. Tracy,
Samuel L. Comstock,   Catharine B. Poole,
Marinda L. Adams,   Ellyette W. Casey,
Ellen A. Evans,   Ellen V. Bowen,
H. Wadsworth Clark.

1857

Theodore Y. Kinne,   Ellen M. Cheney,
Mary J. Hopkins,   Julia A. Hawley,
W. K. Hood.

1858

George K. Collins,   William P. Burdick,
William H. Shankland,   James S. McVey,
Josephine Hurlburt,   Mary A. Morwick,
S. Jennie Marlette,   F. Amelia Clarke.

1859

Charles M. Kinne,   J. Frank Durston,
William Henry Robbins, Clara A. Kingsley,
William G. Tracy,   Eliza M. Riegel,
Margaret Moore,   Mary Jane Shuler,
Helen M. Davis,   Mary E. Fisher,

Sarah A. Corey,   Kate Frazee,
Orpha J. Jones,   Elide A. Cummings.

1860

Jacob A. Nottingham,   Truman J. Backus,
Fillmore M. Smith,   G. Spencer Codington,
Albert Becker,   Mary L. Stevens,
Mary A. Bassett,   Catherine E. Tallman,
Maria Freeland,   Annie D. Phelps,
Emma C. Saul,   Kate E. Dewey,
Nettie Featherly,   Elizabeth I. Palmer,
            Leonard M. Alger.

1861

H. Frank Babcock,   Edson H Wilder,
Smith Northway,   Charles J. Glass,
Henry D. Nottingham,   Andrew W. Wilkins,
Thomas W. Durston,   A. Melinda Gilbert,
Permelia Nottingham,   Louise H. Rose,
Harriet L. Powers,   Harriet W. Beebe,
Eliza G. Chapman,   Mary E. Sheppard,
Emily Jerome,   Mary F. Stevens,
Mary E. Morgan,   Edmonia G. Highgate,
Sarah C. Glass,   Clara F. Chase,
Lola M. Evans,   Catherine M. S. Scanlan,
Avis Stearnes.   Mary L. Beebe,
            Thomas Hooker.

1862

Dudley P. Wilkinson,   Alice B. Barber,
William F. Hubbard,   Louise O. Gere,
H. E. Prindle,   Sarah H. Ecker,
Charles R. White,   Jennie M. Lee,

Ella P. Bates,
Deckie M. Cheesebro,
Annie E. Hayden,
Mary E. Crowen,
Emma J. Ostrander,

M. Frances Stevens,
Florence Stevens,
Lina M. Dwight,
Josephine Magee,
Anna Sager.

1863

Levi C. Lathrop,
Thomas M. Ryan,
Edward N. Westcott,
Alida T. Ketchum,
Emma J. Chase,
Lettie A. Russell,
Louise L. Smith,
Lois A. Heath,
Mary E. Kelley,
Fanny L. Rounds,
Margaret F. Paddock,

George W. Waggoner,
Grace E. Holmes,
Frances A. Hayden,
Frances M. Prindle,
M. E. Brintnall,
Josephine P. Crane,
Ada G. Barnes,
Eliza A. Kennedy,
Catherine M. Marsh,
Julia A. Wescott,
Carrie E. Wescott,

Giles A. Lewis.

1864

Henry C. Cole,
John T. B. Hillhouse,
Albert E. McChesney,
S. H. Starin,
Frances A. Beach,
Agnes E. Usenbentz,

Alice E. Herrick,
Addie C. Thurston,
James W. Lawrence,
M. Elizabeth Van Wagenen,
Julia A. Britcher.

1865

Francis C. Pope,
Lewis F. Powell,
William Davis,
John H. Durston,
Charles Pratt,

DeEtta D. Spear,
Margaret Hurst,
Harriet M. Adams,
Mary R. Vischer,
Emma F. Hood,

Henri Bitter,
Edgar P. Glass,
Alice E. Waters,
Harriet S. Leach,
Sarah C. Terwilliger,

Lucy Truesdell,
Rosella Snow,
Hester A. Leyden,
Ella Hurst,
Frances L. Leonard.

1866

Albert C. Phillips,
Sarah Jerome,
Ida B. Terry,
Frances M. Chesebro,
Winifred Davies,
Alice Ritchie,

Margaret A. Dunn,
M. Elizabeth Terry,
Ella Starin,
Libbie M. Dakin,
Abigail Croly,
Margaret E. Barber,

Wilson R. Hare.

1867

Georgiana Lascelle,
Julia E. Hoye,
Lilly M. Fuller,
Mary E. Gere,

Wealthy Arnold,
Ella M. Chase,
Catherine Celia Murphy,
Theodosia A. Holmes,

Mary D. Hurst.

1868

Horatia S. White,
James L. Thorpe,
Estella Freeman,
Alice E. Fitzgerald,
Eva L. Smith,
Caroline Arntz,
D. Louise Woolworth,
Rhoda Van Wagenen,

John F. Burdick,
Charles J. Powers,
Mary G. Dunn,
Charlotte A. Redhead,
Sarah T. Stafford,
Laura E. Fuller,
Mary D. Baker,
Julia A. Clarke.

1869

James B. Hitchcock,

W. Allen Butler,

William H. Mills,
Mary E. Sykes,
Julia M. Killmore,
Nellie F. Maynard,
Ida L. Hurd,
Orissa A. Hitchcock,
Emma A. Welch,

Mary L. Ford,
Henrietta Hurst,
Mary Silberman,
Emma L. Riegal,
Mary S. Murphy,
Sarah Freeland,
Grace E. Terry,

William H. Barnes.

1870

Willard K. Spencer,
William T. Mylcrane,
James M. Gilbert,
Thomas F. Coolie,
Mary E. Nicholson,
Ella Dickie,
Helen I. Adams,
Agnes L. Lynch,
Mary E. Vaughan,
Ellen Hayden,
E. Augusta Clement,

Brace W. Loomis,
Edward J. Lally,
Orrin J. Snow,
Carrie L. Smith,
Kate W. Johonnot,
Mary E. Hawley,
Catherine A. Nichols,
Isabel E. Warner,
Lucy E. Babcock,
Allena E. Coville,
M. Olivia Sanger.

1871

Clinton J. Peck,
Arthur B. Kinne,
Ferdinand J. Ballart,
William A. Wood,
J. Wiltse Knapp,
Joseph Lally,
James W. Ford,
Henry G. Hanchett.
Ella L. Hayes,
Sarah J. Dallas,
Nellie J. Abbott,

Emma F. Bunnell,
Sophia Straus,
Agnes A. McKeon,
Etta J. Pope,
Lavinia Van Wagenen,
Elizabeth C. Dwyre,
Sara Nutting,
Bessie Holyoke,
Emma G. Soule,
Clara L. Terry,
Sarah Brinkerhoff,

Louise M. Robinson,   Amelia L. Curry,
Margarette B. Leech,   Ella M. Dunn.

1872

William Loguen,   Abby K. Keene,
George F. Hine,   Jennie M. Knapp,
Patrick Cummins,   Mary A. Losacker,
E. Olin Kinne,   Lizzie Rogers,
Edwin Nottingham,   Rachel Stearns,
William S. Nottingham,   Margaret E Stacey,
Albert B. Randall,   Rebecca J. Schemerhorn,
Elwin D. Plaisted,   Mary A. Berney,
Henry F. Thomsen,   Eva L. Williams,
Helen A. Plumb,   Mira Kingsley,
Isabelle S. Usenbentz,   Ella Cole,
Mary Arnold,   Anna Adams,
Ida A. Gilbert,   Mary Hayes,
Florence Chidester,   Ellen Kennedy,
Fanny Hopkins,   Effie L. Curtiss,
Cora A. Britton,   Henriette Clark,
Sara A. Barber,   Emma H. Munger,
Olivia McCann,   Fanny I. Noxon.
Mary Murray,   Josephine McKevitte,
             Emma M. Merrick.

1873

The High school course was changed to a four years' course, and diplomas were given to these on three years' work.

John Hunter,   Mary Logan,
Fred L. Dillaye,   Lillian Burdick,
J. Willis Candee,   Margaret F. Freeland.

1874

William B. Harlow,
Nathan Jacobson,
Louis Marshall,
Edgar J. Mowatt,
Alfred T. Sanford,
Ada M. Beach,
Mary A. Bolway,
M. Lizzie Fairchild,
Marilla Goldstein,
Margaret A. Kelly,
Bessie Lowe,

Agnes McCann,
Susie A. Paine,
Helen M. Post,
Ida A. Roblin,
Alice M. Sitterly,
Ella C. Stanton,
Mary J. Widger,
E. Louise Wright,
Clarence N. Blowers,
Leroy Pharis,
Will Stark.

1875

Horace D. Babcock,
Maltbie B. Babcock,
William C. Bennett,
A. Clifford Mercer,
Alfred Wilkinson, Jr.
Elizabeth J. Bainbridge,
Adella L. Baker,
Minnie A. Barney,
Ida B. Gilbert,
Ida M. Hay,
Margaret Hicks,
Hattie N. Holmes,

Mary A. Lally,
Kittie Leyden,
Jennie R. Ludington,
Mary E. Morse,
Anna J. Nicholson,
Emma F. Nicholson,
Rachel C. Phillips,
Catherine J. Pickard,
Mary Sprole,
Hattie J. Walter,
Elizabeth Weigel,
Amelia Weiskotten.

1876

William D. Andrews,
Daniel F. Curtin,
Rolla S. Helmer,
Frank L. Lyman,
Albert D. Soule,
Edward S. Stevens,

Mary J. Emmons,
Annie F. Fitzgerald,
Catherine N. Hall,
Mary E. Peck,
Alida B. Plant,
Mary F. Prendergast,

Clarence E. Wolcott,
Margaret F. Behan,
Ada A. Brewster,
Clarabel Childs,

M. Anna Robbins
Sarah L. Roney,
Mary A. Shannon,
Annie L. Walsh,

Ella S. Dales.

1877

William W. Wilcox,
Fred H. Howard,
Fred W. Oswald,
Walter R. Bridgeman,
Henry W. Roberts,
Florence E. Herrick,
Emma D. Seifker,
Flora Cole,
Theresa F. Lyons,
Lena Porter,
Lottie E. Bach,
Cora E. Coleman,
Effie A. Didama,
Lizzie M. Foster,
Grace A. Hatfield,
Emeline Kennedy,
Lizzie V. Soule,
Mary B. Dingham,

Elias S. Nutting,
Arthur Baker,
Charles A. F. Thomsen,
Alice M. Wood,
Margaret F. Shannon,
Mary A. Sullivan,
E. Eva Fowler,
Nellie F. Cummings,
Julia E. Quigley,
M. Gussie Booth,
Cornelia L. Crossett,
Sophia E. Elsner,
Lucella R. Hancock,
Amy J. Holmes,
Blanche M. S. McCann,
Florence A. Greenman,
Gertrude B. Harlow,
Ella A. Wyman,

Frank L. Higgins.

FIRST CLASS OF 1878

Will. P. Barber,
Leonard Bronner,
William A. Hawley,
W. Fred Mann,
Peter E. Sheridan,
Samuel E. Sprole,

Anna K. King,
Adella A. Martin,
Nellie F. Packard,
Lizzie B. Smith,
Maggie Smith,
Anna Whitney,

Charlotte S. Henn,
Emma E. Lancaster,
Anna Moriarty,
Sarah M. Sanderson,
Maylon C. Britton,
Isaac H. Crysler,
Julius H. Lowenthal,
Charles T. McChesney,
Colin A. Spaulding,
Ella N. Garlick,

Bessie I. Allen,
Rosa I. Bierhart,
Fanny Colwell,
Emma E. Everding,
Blanche E. Weaver,
Mary H. Abeel,
Eva Ayres,
L. May Cameron,
Laura S. Congdon,
Kittie R. Fairchild.

SECOND CLASS OF 1878

Henry M. Chase,
William A. Gere,
Frank D. Gott,
Joseph Stolz,
Jennie M. Cate,
Clara E. Curry,
Minnie I. Dunford,
Julia F. Farnham,
Anna A. Holsman,
Cora I. Kinyon,
Ida L. Powers,
Mattie E. Smith,
Minnie M. Stone,
Etta C. Gibbs,
Irene C. Hawley,
Elizabeth W. Holliger,
Mary L. Sullivan,
Alice L. Town,

Oscar C. Kinyon,
John G. Sharpe,
Charles C. Sherman,
Julia E. Carroll,
Hattie L. Cole,
J. Frankie Driscoll,
Gussie N. Fairchild,
Minnie C. Foster,
Susie E. Jones,
Susie E. Parsons,
Lavillie F. Sawyer,
Libbie Sprole,
Nellie F. Garfield,
Marion Gott,
Jessie E. Hayden,
Lizzie Sullivan,
Agnes M. Town,
Emma Woods.

FIRST CLASS OF 1879

Amy Campbell,
Lizzie Dunford,

Ida Gilger,
Mamie L. Rose,

Sara M. Maxon,   Abbie Whalen,
Hattie S. Stevens,   Ethel Griffin,
Lutie Wright,   Emma Hopper,
Ada Harris,   Alfred C. Ginty,
Phebe Howlett,   Charles F. Sitterly,
Edwin M. Maxon,   Calvin G. Stevens,
                   Minnie Clarkson.

SECOND CLASS OF 1879

William J. Ayling,   Burt Cowles,
Carlton Curtiss,   William Gannon,
Everard A. Hill,   John H. Humphries,
James E. Mulheran,   Scott Owen,
George I. Post, Jr.,   Lula Brewster,
Katie Dore,   Flora Hawley,
Ina M. Landgraff,   Ella M. Pharis,
Hattie Noxon,   Julia Knight,
Lola A. Salisbury,   Joanna Savage,
Tillie Siefker,   Sarah Smith,
Hattie E. Stevens,   Lydia Thomsen,
Louise B. Upton,   Mary E. Wolz.

FIRST CLASS OF 1880

Annie E. Bainbridge,   Kittie C. Dunn,
Mary E. Duguid,   Celia Ford,
Kittie T. Dunn,   Annie Holkins,
Hattie G. Hanmer,   Della C. Mills,
Frankie W. Manchester,   Charles J. Markert,
Lizzie Miller,   Eva Parker,
Carrie A. Ormsbee,   Carrie M. Rowley,
Nellie A. Rector,   Charles J. Walch,
Ella B. Thompson,   Carrie S. Young,
                   Kittie L. Dwyer.

SECOND CLASS OF 1880

George D. Hammond,
Charles J. Peters,
Frank G. Peters,
E. Irving Rockwell,
E. Josie Balch,
Lizzie Carter,
Grace Collins,
Louise A. Gebhart,
Mary J. McLane,
Marion S. Morss,
Frances S. Van Hoesen,
Edwin J. Seagar,
Samuel Shevelson,
James H. Talbott,
Samuel G. Weiskotten,
Bessie U. Hess,
Kittie E. Kinne,
Mamie A. Kinne,
Tracy A. Lowe,
Mary A. Smith,
Jennie S. Tyler,
Fannie L. Van Hoesen,
Lizette F. Rockwell,
Carrie C. Walsh,
Emma A. D. Lansing.

FIRST CLASS OF 1881

Joseph Bondy,
Edward Cahill,
Bert H. Meads,
Carrie L. Allis,
Louie W. Chope,
Mary B. Featherly,
Florence Howe,
Libbie Kelly,
Mary E. Logan,
Mary Miller,
Aggie B. Morrisey,
Lutie Siefker,
Jesse L. Bronner,
Edwin A. Kingsley,
Willard M. White,
Una A. Bagg,
Annie V. Dunn,
Bertha Freusdorf,
Nellie Jarvis,
Mary W. Lincoln,
Nellie Lott,
H. Della Miller,
Emma Rautenberg,
Frances Whipple.

SECOND CLASS OF 1881

George F. Cole,
Lucien B. Miller,
Frank W. Padgham,
William J. Sauter,
Frank A. Welch,
Fannie M. Blye,
M. Octavia Caven,
Julia A. Cummings,

Newton Smith,
Celia C. Hinman,
Eleanor F. Hogan,
Jessie L. Miller,
Bettie Marshall,
Sarah I. Murray,
May Laura Rae,
Rachel M. Rosenthal,
Louisa F. Sax,
Florence C. Seely,

Lizzie E. Cummings,
Florence M. Coates.
Mary Daly,
Maggie Eustace,
Ida E. Goldman,
Euretta Patterson,
Jennie M. Smith,
Aggie L. Tubbert,
Lula J. Wallace,
Grace E. Willey,

Hattie I. Shultz.

FIRST CLASS OF 1882

Robert H. Jones,
Clarence A. Lonergon,
Bertha M. Bannister,
Lillian S. Barnes,
Julia R. Bresnihan,
Louise Brooks,
Alice E. Coykendall,
Carrie H. Crawford,
Mary T. Delaney,

Adolph G. Velasko,
Honora A. Dunford,
Nelle Ford,
Alice E. Lavington,
Clara Marshall,
Mamie B. Maynard,
Carrie L. Rose,
Minnie E. Smith,
Fannie V. Sprole,

Samuel D. Solomon.

SECOND CLASS OF 1882

George E. Chapman,
Louis M. Howe,
William H. May,
Mary D. Allis,
Adelaide R. Bayette,
Lizzie S. Bridgeford,
Lizzie A. Chope,
Maude Durston,

George M. Price,
Theodore K. Wilkinson,
Mary Rena Harrison,
Mary Hungerford,
Etta Marie Kittell,
Emma Genevieve Lang,
Nellie G. Norton,
Nellie Lucille Randall,

Lottie Irene Earll,
Dora Ettelson,
Marie L. Flach,
Kate Louise Fry,
Arabella W. Cowles,

Katie C. Rogers,
Mary Sharp,
Frankie E. Slattery,
Nettie A. Tomlinson,
Emma A. Freeland,

FIST CLASS OF 1883

Clara Adell Armstrong,
Minnie J. Bidwell,
Lillie C. Carroll,
Julia M. Conroy,
Annie F. Dee,
Minnie E. Duffy,
Grace Greenwood Free-
    man,
Lizzie M. Gannon,
Jennie K. Griffin,
Cora Adella Harrington,
Alice H. Holliday,

Anna M. Hopstein,
Clara Persis Knapp,
Nellie C. Leo,
Lulu Frances Leyden,
Anna Cora Mayo,
Phœbe Alice Sanderson,
Carrie E. Sawyer,
Margaret K. Schneider,
Fanny Sharpe,
Nellie Sloan,
Carleton A. Chase,
Dominick A. Rafferty.

SECOND CLASS OF 1883

Yetta Estelle Bondy,
Kate A. Crawford,
May E. Duncan,
Abbie Madalene Isaacs,
Clara Searing King,
Minnie Louise Overacker,
Anna Rose Shevelson,
Katie Smith,
Addie Belle Talbot,
William Hurd Miller,

James Park Becker,
Ambrose Chas. Driscoll,
Benjamin F. Hammond,
Charles Bryant Johnson,
Charles Francis McFall,
John Earl May,
James Francis Michel,
Edward L. Miller,
Irving Franklyn Baxter,
Hartmann L. Oberlander.

FIRST CLASS OF 1884

Mattie E. Arnold,
Mamie T. Bierhart,

M. Louise Baum,
Geneva M. Brand,

Cora May Bell,
Frankie Gregg,
Kittie Williams,
Pearl Sibson,
Minnie T. Thorne,
Wilber G. Jones,
Benjamin Stolz,

Bertha E. Curtis,
Louise L. Hunt,
Delia T. Keefe,
Clara Smith,
John D. Fogarty,
Frank J. Schnauber,
Carl G. White.

SECOND CLASS OF 1884

George L. Ammerman,
Frank B. Harris,
Nellie L. Auer,
Susie M. Baker,
Kittie L. Bierhart,
Ellen A. Dunn,
May Giddings,
Delia C. Keehner,
George M. McChesney,
Minda Morrison,
Charlotte C. Palmer,
Carrie B. Salmon,
Ruby A. Webb,
George W. Standen,

Thomas B. Fitch,
Frank H. McChesney,
Jessie M. Bagg,
Adeline H. Barnes,
Wilda Chapman,
Lucy Ford,
Jennie T. Kappesser,
Leila M. Kennedy,
Mamie McDonald,
Julia R. Murray,
Della Rosenthal,
Rachel Shevelson,
Grace C. Williams,
Mary E. Abbott.

FIRST CLASS OF 1885

Anna L. Barton,
Ida M. Cooley,
Etta Levi,
Nera Power,
Julia W. Stephens,
Horace W. Britcher,
William B. Crowley,
Bert R. Hall,

Kate L. Clark,
Lizzie S. Emens,
Katherine F. Murray,
Louisa Smith,
Anna P. Terry,
Morris W. Chase,
Simon L. Elsner,
William Jenney,

Arthur E. Parsons,
Herman W. Tamkin,
Charles P. Lynch,
Oscar R. Whitford,
John Wilkinson.

SECOND CLASS OF 1885

Charles S. Chesebrough,
Nelson P. Snow,
Thomas Turnbull, Jr.,
Annie H. Agan,
Louis Barnes,
Minnie Davis,
M. Louise Dennison,
Minnie H. Freeoff,
Clara E. Greenley,
Julia A. Levy,
Ellen Murray,
Florence A. Sherwood,
Josephine Williams,
Charles A. Gwynn,
Noble E. Whitford,
William H. Nicholson,
Mary A. Bagg,
May L. Cuyler,
Maggie F. Delany,
Louise Ford,
Louisa B. Gere,
Kittie Lewis,
Carrie B. Mills,
Martha M. Schultze,
Mollie Willett,
Florence A. Wright.

FIRST CLASS OF 1886

Charles F. Diel,
George Henry Williamson,
Edward Ashley Gray,
Julia Isabel Lamphier,
Nellie Augusta Carroll,
Clara Loomis Skiff,
Elizabeth K. Loos,
Nellie A. Rellis,
Theresa Gutstadt,
Mary Eva Gannett,
Jessie Leona Hollenbeck,
Mary Zella Andrews,
Lucy S. Bainbridge,
Nellie R. Bainbridge,
Una E. Bierhart,
Marie Louise Denison,
Clara Daisy Sanford,
Clara Levy,
Libbie C. Markell,
Hattie Jacobson,
Lydia A. Prudhon,
Ida Marshall,
Cora Schoener,
Frances Eva Worden,
Mamie Leary,
E. Belle Livermore,
Minnie L. Crow.

SECOND CLASS OF 1886

D. Bruce Kennedy,
Philip D. Schuyler,
Mitchell C. Harrison,
Theodore A. Foster,
John C. Shoudy,
Louis Gould,
Etta H. Avery,
Ella H. Cook,
Aggie May Gannett,
Ada A. Knapp,

Hannah R. Richford,
Mary A. O'Brien,
Nellie A. Ryan,
Augusta C. Baumgrass,
Hattie L. Stackhouse,
Grace D. Clarke,
Florence A. Larrabee,
Grace L. Duncan,
Mamie Smith,
Clara M. Sweet,

Lillian V. Moser.

FIRST CLASS OF 1887

Curtis Niles Andrews,
Blanche Beatrice Bannan,
Florence Adah Barton,
Rosemary Baum,
Estelle Grace Britton,
Sarah Porter Brown,
Annabel Brumelkamp,
Marcia Aurilla Carpenter,
Walter Barnes Cherry,
Florence Belle Collins,
Sara Isabel Cummins,
Elizabeth Grace Dowling,
Alveretta Falvey,

Mary Ellen Gere,
Gates Hamburger,
Mary Abigail Ingham,
Elizabeth Louise Kieffer,
Frank Land,
Mary Elizabeth McGowan
Annie McMahon,
Mary Moyer,
Richard J. O'Donnell,
Mary Sophia Pitkin,
Nina Louise Sawyer,
Lulu Marie Tickner,
Minnie Elizabeth Wescott

Brinna Finkelstein.

SECOND CLASS OF 1887

Edward S. Allis,
Kate L. Abbott,
Nellie L. Abbott,

Harriet B. Hopkins,
Harriet A. Humbert,
Myra I. Husted,

Theresa L. Bannan,
Mary A. Boggs,
Evalyn Boldry
Ellen J. Casey,
Blanche H. Colman,
Julia M. Cook,
Hiram B. Danziger,
Eleanor V. Delancy,
Rose M. Delaney,
Emma A. Elsner,
Anna P. Ferris,
Grace L. Ferris,
Genevra Gwynn,
Martha N. Hayden,
Lillian M. Heath,
Laura E. Hickok,

H. Howell Kennedy,
Louis P. Lang,
Anna A. Lynch,
Anna L. Mack,
Ina Mercer,
Eleanor L. Orr,
Cora M. Pierce,
John W. Plant,
Bertha S. Sawyer,
Jennie V. Sheldon,
Sarah Silverstein,
Louie V. Snell,
John E. Sullivan,
Anna F. Warner,
Nina Weston,
Jessie A. Williams,

Mary L. Wood.

FIRST CLASS OF 1888

Frank Ludington Ames,
Herman J. Bierhart, Jr.,
Edmund L. French,
Frederick Charles Baird,
Edward Howard Dann,
Clarence Leslie Hewitt,
Edwin Phillips Lyman,
Beardsley N. Sperry,
Ethel Clara Berry.
Isadore Adell Blanden,
Etta Ettelson,
Grace Whitney Leslie.

Bridget Agnes Lynch,
Mary Stanley,
Emma Carrie Woese,
Eugene Fritz McKinley,
Jeremiah H. Sullivan,
Mary Chapman Bennett,
Mary Francesca Breen,
Amelia Raymond Hough,
Hattie Lesser,
Margaret V. Rogers,
Mollie Trowbridge,
Jessie Æolia Whyborn.

SECOND CLASS OF 1888

George Morgan Bacon,
Charles R. Bardeen,

Bridget A. Dewan,
Jennie Dietz,

William E. Beeman,
Theodore W. Clark,
George N. Cooper,
George T. Head,
John J. McCarthy,
Elliot Judd Northrup,
Philip F. Schneider,
William M. Shirley,
William H. Smith,
Joseph C. Walier,
Charles F. Wiley,
Etta Bolger,
Myrtie E. Brewster,
Nina Burpee,
Edith Cornwell,
Emma Davey,
Mamie E. DeLano,

Mamie F. Dwyer,
Margaret E. Evans,
May Fayle,
Minnie M. Gothier,
Rose M. Hall,
Hattie C. Hedden,
Alvia Horton,
Grace M. Howe,
Matie A. Keehner,
Anna L. Mackey,
Edith Palmer,
Lydia Reiss,
Bertha Schott,
Gail Sherman,
Bertha E. Steiger,
M. Hattie Tanguay,
Minnie Traugott.

FIRST CLASS OF 1889

Carl Bacon,
D. A. Blum,
James L. Brewer,
E. C. Britcher,
Raymond E. Clapp,
John H. Cook,
C. Arthur Church,
Peter Drum,
George J. Dunham,
Hiram W. Eastman,
William P. Graham,
Willard A. Hirsch,
Robert E. Keeler,
Frank J. Miller,
Clarence Perry,

Belle L. Dicks,
May Earll,
Eva L. Everingham,
Jessie Fish,
Agnes Ford,
Sarah L. Hanley,
Florence Hanna,
Margaret L. Hollister,
Jennie L. Hopkins,
Marguerite E. Kelly,
Eva King,
Mabel A. Potter,
Josie L. Reddy,
Mary Ryan,
Josie Sager,

Katharine Allis,
Emma Alvord,
Sophia Bloom,
Lizzie Brassel,
Nellie W. Buckley,
Laura M. Buss,

Frances Schillinger,
Mabel Stone,
Grace G. Truair,
Grace H. Webb,
M. Louise Whedon,
Josephine Wilkins,

Mabelle A. Clark.

SECOND CLASS OF 1889

William J. Gere,
Louis W. Hall,
Bert E. Larkin,
J. Burnett Nash,
William Rubin,
Daniel F. Salmon,
B. Robinson Schenck,
Harry Silverstein,
Lorin A. Swarthout, Jr.,
Ernest I. White,
Florence J. Beecler,
Nellie M. Behan,
Hattie J. Caldwell,
Ida V. Cassidy,
Flora B. Collins,
Stella Danziger,
Lulu A. Day,
Lillian DeLong,
Libbie E. Dills,
Allen G. Tripp,

Helene Dixson,
Jessie Grant,
Gratia Gwynn,
Margaret Hayden,
Julia V. Helmer,
Julia Latterner,
Minnie Lenehan,
Mary Louise Leonard,
Anna D. Mara,
Mary Pharis,
Blossom Rill,
Mary E. Ryan,
Elizabeth Schneider,
Lizzie Sedgwick,
Charlotte S. Stone,
Daisy Tallman,
Edith Truair,
Cornelia White,
Aggie Wood,
William Wheatley, Jr.

FIRST CLASS OF 1890

George W. Barnes,
Charles W. Beadel,

Agnes D. Mulheran,
Mary G. O'Donnell,

George H. Bond,
Harry Brill,
Irving M. Bronner,
A. H. Cowie,
J. Alfred Diel,
Henry E. Dills,
Fred J. Haynes,
W. J. Leslie,
F. S. Lighthall,
J. R. McGowan,
Daniel Pratt,
Eva C. Earll,
Mary E. Gallavin,
Lillian F. Hamilton,
Jennie Gray Harrington,
Clementine Helfer,
May McCulloch,
Elizabeth J. Morris,
Sadie J. Moulter,

Anna Pakelnisky,
Carrie E. Parshall,
Sallie Pratt,
Ed. J. Reddington,
George O. Reddington,
Adna W. Risley,
Frank A. Rosenthal,
Bert E. Salisbury,
Ed. S. Van Duyn,
Addie L. Clark,
Dena B. Draper,
Emma Ryan,
Mabel D. Searl,
Carrie Schuyler,
Augusta Smith,
Bertha Stripple,
Tassie Sullivan,
Mary E. Tobin,
Lena F. Weisburg.

SECOND CLASS OF 1890

Harry T. Babcock,
William B. Chase,
Fayette K. Congdon,
Mansfield J. French,
Clarence N. Goodwin,
Harry Neal Hyde,
William Lester,
Frank W. Noxon,
Minnie E. Curtis,
Gertrude R. Danziger,
Madge B. Dietz,
Anna F. Erwin,

Rebecca Amdursky,
Pearl E. Belding,
Nellie Brennan,
Emma Elizabeth Brown,
Jennie B. Chope,
Maud S. Coan,
Mary A. Collins,
Jennie S. Cook,
Sarah Crabtree,
Nellie J. Gifford,
Emily J. Goulding,
Mary Estelle Hamson,

Anna Fahey,
Grace M. Featherly,
Jennie Gebhart,
Lucie A. Genzel,
William F. Rafferty,
Charles W. Reussow,
J. W. Stevens,
John G. Truair,
Waldo Weston,
George M. White,
Belle Adams,

Milicent A. Hinkley,
Victoria M. Kemter,
Edith M. Lawrence,
Ella Leary,
Edith M. Lyon,
Lena I. Manson,
Katherine Packard,
Ida Rosman,
Rachel Solomon,
Katherine S. Throop,
Irene M. Timmons,

Florence E. Trowbridge.

FIRST CLASS OF 1891

George E. Boschert,
Charles J. Brown,
Thomas U. Chesebrough,
Henry J. Clark,
John T. DeLaney,
James F. Foley,
Edward H. Hungerford,
Henry Philip James,
Frank B. Lord,
Samuel Pakelnishky,
Ludlow H. Smith,
S. Holt Starin,
Walter R. Stone,
Carrie E. Allen,
Nora Francis Dillon,
Anna E. Gardner,
Florence L. Grumbach,
Mary Louise Hubbard,
Maud Kinsley,
E. Maud Lewis,

Katherine L. O'Keefe,
Alice Meade Palmer,
Ella Passmore,
Mary L. Pendergast,
Lucy M. Plumb,
Carrie E. Anderson,
Mary E. S. Babcock,
Bertha Foote Bardeen,
Carrie E. Beeler,
Mabel E. Boomer,
Emma A. Borgwardt
Lulu Adelle Bunnell,
Kate A. Concannon,
Joanna Cotter,
Mabel DeLong,
Anna McCullock Rich,
Carrie A. Ritter,
Lena Rogers,
Charlotte F. Ross,
Mary E. Salmon,

May Lindemer,
Alta May Matteson,
Mary Libbie McConnell,
Clara Grace McKinstry,
Coletta C. Young.

Fannie M. Sherwood,
A. Lillian M. Smith,
Ada L. Sunderlin,
Eva M. Yorker,

SECOND CLASS OF 1891

Louise C. Adams,
Mabel Hurd,
Clara K. Harth,
Henrietta E. Blanden,
Agnes E. Cahill,
Cora T. Danziger,
Emma A. Davis,
Theresa L. DeForest,
Leila B. Durston,
Adella C. Farrington,
Lizzie F. Foley,
Carrie L. Ford,
Agnes C. Gannon,
Laura A. Herzog,
Ada E. Humbert,
Florence A. Huntley,
Nellie Joy,
Lillian Judson,
Laura D. Kaufman,
Marion Kinsley,
Eva D. Levy,
Estelle L. McCoy,
Tillie Miller,
May Moore,
Kittie A. Nicholson,
Bessie Parsons,

Theresa W. Sharkey,
Leora E. Sherwood,
Grace L. Spoor,
Harriet B. VanDenburg,
Kittie A. Walsh,
Gertrude E. Weller,
Edward Blum,
John J. Buettner,
Peter B. Cole,
William J. Cushing,
William B. Dow,
Samuel I. Ferguson,
Fred W. Hammond,
Don A. Hollister,
Haswell C. Jeffery,
Edward H. Kraus,
Milton M. Leiter,
David R. Leslie,
Michael M. Lucid,
Howard C. Mills,
Edwin B. Mott,
Edward K. Mundy,
John A. Nichols,
David W. Nicholson,
Edwin W. Parsons,
Fred T. Pierson,

Katherine E. Peabody,
Minnie A. Quinlan,
Sarah R. Rogers,
Joseph C. Seiter,
George A. Smith,
Joseph F. Tebeau,
J. Henry Walters.

FIRST CLASS OF 1892

Carrie Annable,
Agnes Behan,
Kittie E. Brogan,
Mary L. Caldwell,
May Candee,
Julia E. Church,
Julia A. Eagan,
Lena Frazier,
Beulah S. Gaylord,
Hattie E. Gould,
Nellie I. Grant,
Grace M. Green,
Minnie Hogan,
Cora E. Kennedy,
Margaret G. Kimball,
Mamie E. Lynch,
Ada L. Manchester,
Carrie Manson,
Louise A. McClure,
Mary Munro,
Susie Over,
Estella E. Padgham,
Helen Potter,
Minnie A. Strauss,
Georgia Wilson,
Katie M. Zimmer,
George S. Avery,
George B. Beach,
John W. Church,
Chester Clark,
Joseph Feinberg,
William E. Hewitt,
Theodore Kieffer,
John S. Lewis,
Elisha J. D. Melhinch,
Fred Morgan,
Peter Schlosser,
Max Umbrecht,
Irving D. Vann,
Henry G. White.

SECOND CLASS OF 1892

Moses Altman,
Charles A. Comerford,
Will L. Day,
J. David Enright,
George A. Hanford,
Blanche Gillette,
D. May Goodrich,
Alice R. Graves,
Edith B. Hall,
Ida W. Harth,

James L. Herrick,
Clinton L. Hodges,
Marx L. Holstein,
Charles W. Kelly,
Clarence D. Kingley,
Charles A. Mack,
Frank E. Miller,
Harvey W. Miller,
Maurice Pakelnishky,
Darwin F. Pickard,
Elmer J. Scott,
G. Frank Tyrrell,
Edwin T. Whiflin,
Charles E. White,
Fred B. Wilbur,
Earll W. Wilson,
George Zahm,
Bertha Ackerman,
Rose Ackerman,
Gertrude L. Andrews.
Eola Bagg.
Nellie A. Baird,
Grace E. Bell,
Nina M. Boynton,
Clara E. Brockway,
Charis L. Carroll,
Eloise S. Cool,
Carrie L. Crysler,
Elizabeth S. Dixson,
Mary S. Ecker,
Satie Frensdorf,
Kittie B. Gallavin,

Cornelia B. Haynes,
Cora E. Haywood,
Fredericka B. Horner,
Mary F. Johnson,
Clara M. Jones,
Libbie Keeffe,
Margarite E. Lodge,
Mary E. Lonergon,
Louise Maloney,
Marian McAllister,
Mabel M. McClure,
Maggie McGraw,
Carlotte J. Mitchell,
Edna A. Myers,
Grace D. Newton,
Edith M. Packard,
Lillie Ransom,
Hattie Rashkower,
Besse Byan,
Josephine F. Shanahan,
Mabel C. Stackhouse,
Lena E. Tappan,
Margaret E. Telford,
Leah Tallman,
Sura Tumin,
Ethel C. Ward,
Kate E. Warner,
Rose B. Webb,
Alice Weston,
May Wheatley,
Bessie M. Willard,
Mabel L. Willard,

Louise V. Winfield.

www.ingramcontent.com/pod-product-compliance
Lightning Source LLC
Chambersburg PA
CBHW021112270326
41929CB00009B/839